A–Z Guide to cleaning
and renovating antiques

Tom Rowland

A–Z Guide to cleaning and renovating antiques

Constable London

First published in Great Britain 1981
by Constable and Company Ltd
10 Orange Street London WC2H 7EG
Copyright © 1981 by Tom Rowland
Reprinted 1982
ISBN 0-09-463630-3
Set in Times New Roman 9pt
by Inforum Ltd Portsmouth
Printed in Great Britain by
Ebenezer Baylis & Son Ltd
The Trinity Press, Worcester, and London

Contents

How to use this book

This book is arranged in alphabetical order in three sections.

Section One gives directions on the care of the most common categories of COLLECTABLE ANTIQUES. It deals with simple cleaning and care, and the simpler technicalities of specialist renovation and repair.

Section Two lists all the **materials** recommended for cleaning and repairing, together with details of their specialised uses, availability and sources of supply where they are not to be found in high street shops.

Section Three gives a list of useful addresses of specialised suppliers, and references to this are indicated by an * in Sections One and Two.

Cross-references to Section One are indicated by CAPITALS, and to Section Two by **bold type**.

Introduction

Many collectors of antiques lack both high dexterity or special work-rooms to undertake major restorations to their treasures. Nevertheless they take great pleasure in cleaning and polishing them, and often need to know more about modern methods and materials. In fact, minor repairs, too, can often be undertaken with the minimum of tools by the non-expert, without inflicting damage to their antiques.

This volume provides the reader with detailed information on the most suitable materials to use, and how to apply them. Often the best materials are not known because they are not widely advertised brand-named products; or they can only be got direct from the makers, or from specialist distributors. In this book I have brought together all this information so as to make it readily available to the amateur collector.

Today a host of excellent materials are at hand. They may cost more than mixing your own – although I have included some simple recipes you can make yourself – but the manufacturers have spent time and research on perfecting their product and can certainly exert a greater control over quality and uniformity than can the amateur.

A common mistake made by beginners is being mean over the use of expensive materials. While there is no need to waste, be liberal where necessary.

Another common error is to give up too soon. Ninety per cent of any job is preparatory; the true effect is only revealed in the final stages, sometimes in the last few minutes. It is all too easy to become discouraged, to think you have made a botch of it – and thus to finish in a slapdash manner. Remember, particularly while you are gaining confidence, to be patient – and to be thorough in the preparatory work. If, for instance, you fail to remove the last traces of old varnish before starting to build up a new finish, no amount of polishing will conceal those tell-tale traces.

Before jumping straight into a job pause for a minute to consider what you are going to do. First, if you want to gain confidence and experience, do *not* start on that valuable and irreplaceable treasure that needs attention. The golden rule is, *when in doubt take advice*. A good source is one of the specialists at your local museum; but they are busy people, so concentrate on the specialist problems – and save the others for a friendly antique dealer. But remember, you do not have to pass examinations to become a dealer; some of them do not have much expertise – but may be reluctant to admit their ignorance! However, I'm sure you will find that most restorers will be glad to advise you on what can safely be undertaken.

You, of course, are the best judge of your own competence, but do not be too timid; remember that experts come expensive and there is much you can do yourself.

Before embarking on any process, carry out a small experiment on a hidden or less visible part of the article. Often one cannot tell what lies beneath a dirty or over-painted surface. A gentle scratching with a penknife will often reveal an unsuspected surface below. Don't be like the man who bought a pine-cased grandfather clock which had been painted brown. He immediately removed the offending paint with a stripper – only to discover, too late, that between the bare wood and the paint were the remains of a fine black lacquer Chinese design: he had cleaned off several hundred pounds' worth of value!

Some do's and don'ts
1. Some of the materials discussed are flammable or volatile. These are marked with a symbol 🔥 to indicate they are dangerous. Make sure there are no naked flames or radiant stoves nearby – and don't smoke while using them.
2. Ensure that all products are clearly labelled and dated – some lose their strength with the passage of time.
3. Work in a well ventilated and lighted area.
4. Never dispose of toxic or flammable residues down a drain. Wrap them well in old papers and put them in the dustbin.
5. Where appropriate, wear protective clothing – particularly goggles if you are using powered tools.
6. Always put the tops back on bottles and tins. They can too easily be knocked over.

Section One:
Items to be cleaned and repaired

Contents

Contents

Contents

Contents

Contents

Contents

Contents

ALABASTER

A form of precipitated and compressed gypsum, usually white and translucent, it is the compression which accounts for the veins alabaster usually carries. A similar variety comes from the Eastern Mediterranean, often in pieces of great antiquity.

Both forms will take a high polish. Colours vary from white, yellow, pink and mid-brown, while the veins can be multicoloured but are often green or black. Alabaster is fairly soft, hence easy to carve – and easily scratched. It was much used in ancient Greece, Crete and Egypt for statues and portrait plaques. It is still produced in Near Eastern and Mediterranean countries to make a variety of artefacts.

Usually a wipe-over with a soft cloth dipped in white spirit will clean off surface grime. Acids, present in many types of water, can damage alabaster so when stains persist and a stronger cleaner is called for, be sure to use distilled water in the solution. Try a pad of cotton-wool soaked in Steradent and a fairly hot solution of water. If stains persist use Bell 167 Cleaner and degreaser which is very effective. Only as a last resort, try one of the **paint strippers** such as Nitromors.

Repairs of breaks may be made with P.V.A. or Epoxy Resin **adhesives**. Where there are missing chips or small pieces, the areas can be filled with a paste made of Epoxy Resin adhesive and Kaolin, Whiting or Titanium Oxide **fillers**. All these materials are white powders of different degrees of whiteness and should be selected to tone with the rest of the article. Do not worry too much if you fail to get an exact match; it will look like one of the natural faults in the alabaster.

Once you are satisfied that you have cleaned and restored the article to an acceptable standard, protect the surface with a light application of wax furniture polish.

ALUMINIUM

This silvery, malleable metal is of fairly recent general use. It was known as a precious curiosity as far back as the time of Elizabeth I (her treasury included an aluminium teaspoon 'valued above all else'). But it was not made in any quantity until 1855, when it was shown at the Paris Exhibition. Produced in France at great cost for the next 30 years, in 1886 modern techniques dramatically reduced manufacturing costs.

Aluminium is attacked by caustic preparations, so take care not to expose it to them. The surface is frequently dyed in a variety of colours – that is, anodised – a process much used for industrial labels, fascias, etc.

Because it is such a soft metal, the use of any but the mildest abrasives will cause damage to mirror-, anodised- and patterned-finishes. Corrosion is produced by oxidization, which leaves a hard white deposit. Wipe anodised and mirror finishes with a damp cloth to clean. Use a fine wire wool to burnish matt surfaces, and apply a **wax polish** to protect and enhance the appearance.

Where persistent stains and corrosion are present soak in a laundry Borax solution (1 tablespoon in $\frac{1}{2}$ pint water), but use it cautiously, since further destruction of the surface could result. If further treatment is called for, try one of the fine **abrasives**, such as Jeweller's rouge, Crocus powder, Tripoli powder, fine Emery powder and Whiting, available either in powder or block form.

AMBER

Amber is the fossilised resin from an extinct variety of pine tree. It often contains petrified flower and insect parts, even small whole flies, which are of course much sought after. It is easy to carve and polish and is often employed in the manufacture of jewellery and *objets d'art*. If rubbed with woollen cloth, static electricity is generated, and such things as fluff, scraps of paper and dust are attracted, much as a magnet attracts iron filings. Rubbing also generates a pleasant faint odour of pine forests, with a hint of musk. It has always been credited with magical and therapeutic qualities and certainly its lustre and brilliance improve with constant wear or handling. It is a very beautiful material and deserves to be looked after with loving care. The smell is important, as it is one of the ways of differentiating amber from plastic imitations, which can be very realistic, right down to the embedded flies and flower seeds. A drop or so of ether on the object will also give an indication of genuine amber; the synthetic material will melt and become cloudy on the

How to clean a piece of amber

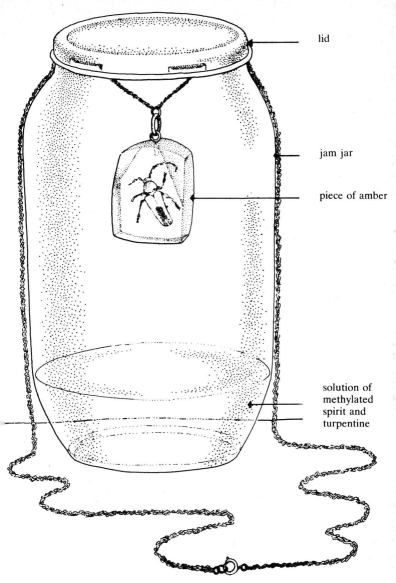

lid

jam jar

piece of amber

solution of
methylated
spirit and
turpentine

suspended with twine, thread or chain

surface. There are two distinct varieties of amber: honey-coloured –
the most common – and a darker brown shade, much the same as
tortoise-shell.

It is normally translucent, but often becomes opaque through
exposure to damp; it should therefore never be washed in water.
Remove dirt by rubbing with French chalk on a soft chamois-leather
or cotton cloth. The opacity can usually be removed by keeping the
article in a warm, moisture-free atmosphere – but take care not to
overheat.

If this treatment is not effective, try suspending the piece above –
but not immersed in, or even touching – a mixture of 1 part
methylated spirit 🔥 and 3 parts artist's turpentine. After
treatment, polish the surface with a wax polish.

Stick broken amber pieces together again, virtually invisibly, with
a single drop of one of the new, instant **adhesives**, such as
Cyanoacrylate Ester adhesive or Epoxy Resin adhesive.

ANTLERS
These collect dust because they are usually placed out of reach. A
thorough blow with an air hose at the local garage will help. Failing
this, a vacuum cleaning followed by a wash over with methylated
spirit on a soft duster will clear all superficial dirt. Polish the horns
with wax polish. If the horns are joined and the boss is covered with
fur or skin, this should be treated with a permanent moth-proofing
agent such as Lindane in either powder or liquid form. Insectidal
powders can be dusted on and worked into the fur. Liquid
insecticides should be sprayed on (see **Insecticides**).
See also HORN and STUFFED ANIMALS.

APPLIQUE
The technique of attaching pieces of fabric to a background
material, so producing a pattern is one of the oldest types of
embroidery known. It may have been invented by the Chinese and
examples have been discovered in both Egyptian and Manchurian
excavations.

Three-dimensional embroidery, known as 'stump work' was
produced in large quantities during the reigns of Charles I and II.

Heavily padded 'pictures' in relief, they are often of rural scenes, worked in buttonhole stitch and sometimes wired round the edges. Human and animal figures are also featured, the heads sometimes carved from wood and covered in cloth, the features then being painted on. This type of decoration was used on all kinds of boxes, mirrors and small pieces of furniture.

Cleaning such items presents considerable problems, because of their possible fragility, non-fastness of colours, unevenness of surface, and attachment to wooden bases.

Considerable quantities of dust and dirt can be removed by vacuum cleaning with a suitable nozzle. It is not difficult to construct or devise a suitable nozzle from rigid plastic or cardboard sheet and self-adhesive tape. But take care that the suction is not so great that the material is damaged or that parts are sucked off.

When cleaning cotton or linen materials, always wash in distilled or soft water. Immersion for several hours, with several changes of water, but no detergent or soap, will remove most ingrained dirt. Fragile materials should be supported by tacking with large stitches to nylon net (to avoid tearing).

First test the fabrics for colour fastness. Damp an unobstrusive area and press between two sheets of blotting paper (white) or cotton sheeting to ensure that there is no leaching of the colour. This test will also reveal if the cloth has been dressed with a non-permanent finish of any kind which would be removed by immersion in water.

Remove bad grease and oily stains by placing two or three layers of blotting paper over the mark and pressing with a warm iron. This will transfer the grease onto the paper and lift it out of the material. An alternative is to make a poultice of Fuller's earth (see **cleaning agents**) with a small amount of water (just enough to bind it together). Apply this to the stain for a few hours and, when it is dry, brush the residue away carefully.

If stains persist, try a dry cleaner: either Trichlorethane or Carbon Tetrachloride 🔥 **solvents** are the best ones to use. Where possible the material should be immersed in the liquid for about fifteen minutes. Where this is not practical, dabbing with a clean cotton pad is the only possible method. Care must be taken that tide rings do not develop at the edges of treated areas, and that the dyes are fast. When working with volatile solvents good ventilation is absolutely vital.

ARMS AND ARMOUR – see WEAPONS AND FIREARMS

BALLPOINT PEN STAINS

Unless action is taken immediately these may become irremovable. Apply methylated spirit 🔥 with a cloth pad. (WARNING: Methylated spirit may melt or damage some synthetic materials which are acetate-based.) Ballpoint pen stains cannot be removed from paper satisfactorily. A **stain remover** like Oxalic acid will remove them from furniture by rubbing hard with wire wool.

BAMBOO

Bamboo furniture has enjoyed vogues of popularity from time to time. In Sheraton's *Cabinet Dictionary* (1803), bamboo is mentioned as a material for chair construction, and imitation bamboo furniture of the late eighteenth century, made from turned beech, painted and coloured to resemble bamboo, can be mistaken for the real article, so accurate is the simulation. Victorian bamboo pieces are considered to be collectors' pieces, fetching surprisingly high prices at auction.

Clean bamboo by scrubbing it with warm, soapy water and a nail brush. Dry carefully and treat with transparent wax polish. Alternatively, coat it with a clear Polyurethane **lacquer** to give more permanent protection and help to arrest splintering.

Bamboo (a form of dried grass) does not break in the same way as wood but it does splinter. When this happens, support the break by inserting a suitably sized length of dowel in the hollow centre of the cane. This may involve cutting the cane, and the best place to do this is at one of the nodules where the cut will be invisible. Drill a suitable hole deep enough to allow the dowel to extend into the next section of the cane. Using as an **adhesive** either Cascamite or a similar Urea Formaldehyde adhesive (which has body as well as gluing properties) – replace the mended sections in position and hold in place with Sellotape while the glue dries.

How to repair a split in bamboo

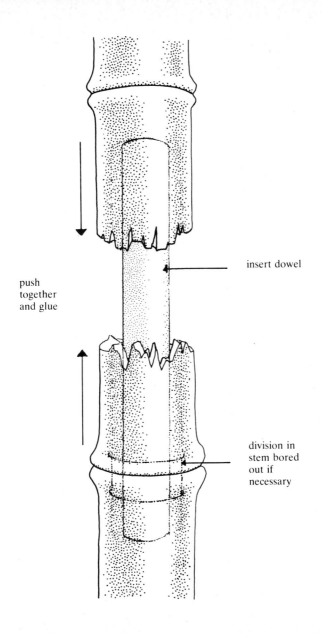

insert dowel

push
together
and glue

division in
stem bored
out if
necessary

When dry, remove the sellotape binding and rub down with a fine sandpaper – clean off, then wax polish or coat with a clear Polyurethane lacquer.

BAROMETERS

There are four types of barometer. The first was invented by Evangelista Torricelli in 1643, and its manufacture quickly spread throughout Europe. It consisted of a column of mercury enclosed in a glass tube, the open end standing in a reservoir open to the atmosphere. However, early improvements in design were essential to make it possible to move them without spilling the mercury The second type was the Syphon barometer, which became the well-known Banjo barometer when a dial was added; Robert Hooke first put the words 'rain', 'change', 'fair', 'set fair', etc. on a dial. The third is the Stick barometer, invented by Jean Fortin (1750–1831). The fourth variety is the Aneroid barometer, invented by Lucien Vidi in 1844.

The first three types of barometer were fitted with one or more scales which could have been of silvered brass, ivory, parchment or even porcelain. While damaged and tarnished scale plates certainly can be resilvered, you should first consider whether you are improving the look, which in turn will depend on the extent of the deterioration of the rest of the instrument. In the case of a badly neglected barometer, it is wise to invest in a complete overhaul by a specialist. The best known in London is Garner and Marney Ltd*, who also supply all barometer parts.

The *Syphon* barometer consists of a U-tube with one arm about a yard long, closed at the end, and one short arm 3–4 ins long, open to the atmosphere. The mercury-filled tube has a glass weight floating on the surface, connected by a silk cord running over a pulley to another, smaller, counter-balance weight. The pulley is fitted with an indicator needle which rotates as the level of the mercury rises and falls with the variation in atmospheric pressure, indicating changes in the weather.

Because of the open-ended tube in this type of barometer, it cannot be laid flat without the mercury escaping. It must always be supported at an angle of 45 degrees (face down) when the

Three different types of barometer

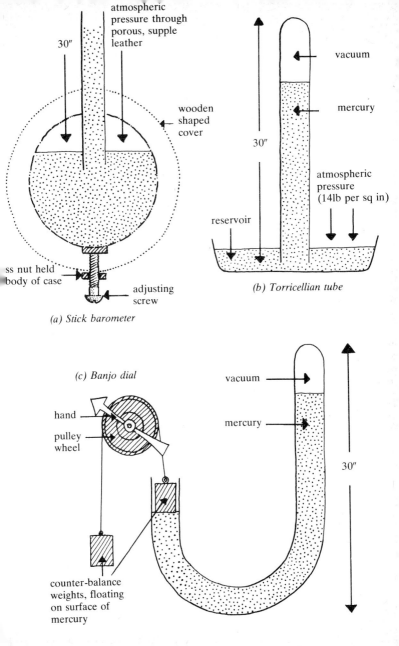

30″

atmospheric
pressure through
porous, supple
leather

wooden
shaped
cover

ss nut held
body of case

adjusting
screw

(a) Stick barometer

vacuum

mercury

30″

atmospheric
pressure
(14lb per sq in)

reservoir

(b) Torricellian tube

(c) Banjo dial

hand

pulley
wheel

counter-balance
weights, floating
on surface of
mercury

vacuum

mercury

30″

mechanism is inspected or cleaned. A sticking needle or pointer usually means that dirt has built up in the tube, preventing the glass weight from moving freely. The weight must be withdrawn carefully and wiped with a duster moistened with a solvent such as methylated spirit. Make sure that the tube is free from dirt and grit before replacing the weight; then repeat the process with the counter-balance weight which is usually enclosed in a similar tube to restrict its movement. Do not attempt to remove or otherwise interfere with the column of mercury. This is a job for a specialist instrument maker. If the case also requires attention, remember that it may not be laid flat. This makes polishing and repairing the wooden parts difficult.

Most barometers are inlaid with patterned stringing. When parts of this decoration are missing, see BEADING AND STRINGING.

The *Stick* barometer is much more robust and easy to transport. Instead of a U-tube, the open end of the column stands in a reservoir of mercury contained in a leather bag. At the base of the reservoir is a brass screw; when tightened, it raises the column of mercury to the top of the tube, so that the instrument can be moved with safety.

In the *Aneroid* barometer, the variation in atmospheric pressure is recorded by a sensitive metal diaphragm covering a circular metal vessel containing a partial vacuum. Slight variations in pressure cause a spring and a gear train to turn the recording pointer. Should an aneroid barometer go wrong, it is likely to be a failure in the vacuum of the pressure vessel; repairs should be done by a specialist.

Remember, these are all delicate scientific instruments. *Always* consult a specialist when in doubt.

Mercury is a poisonous material. Care must be taken when handling it to ensure that it is not swallowed or heated above normal room temperature.

BASKETWORK
Basketwork is made of woven willow, osier wands or twigs. It should not be confused with canework.

Remove dirt and dust with warm water and yellow soap: use a

scrubbing brush or other stiff brush and finish up with a good hosing down, with a pressure jet. Badly discoloured basketwork can be bleached with a diluted household bleach or with Peroxide of Hydrogen.

Old basketwork becomes dry and brittle and in consequence loses its flexibility and breaks. Glue together with acrylic or P.V.A. **adhesive**. Where areas are missing, they can be repaired by weaving in suitable twigs of either willow or hazel. They are, of course, dry when bought from a handicraft supplier, so soak them well for an hour or so in tepid water.

Where basketwork is incorporated in antique furniture, and has deteriorated with wear and tear, it is usually best to replace it completely. A few professional rush and cane workers can still be found. Try your local association for the blind or your county CoSIRA* organiser.

After cleaning or repairing, leave the article to dry thoroughly and then either polish with wax polish, using a clean boot brush or give it a protective coat of Polyurethane lacquer. You will need to tone down new wickerwork on antique furniture; so give it a coat of suitably coloured **wood stain**, or treat with tinted wax polish.

BAYONETS – see WEAPONS

BEADING AND STRINGING

Beadings and mouldings are thin strips of wood that are applied to furniture, either for decoration or to cover up joints. Beadings are plain strips of wood, while mouldings are shaped or carved. Stringing refers to a fine line inlay of wood. By their very nature, they lend themselves to damage as they are most vulnerable to catching on clothing or dusters, or being splintered during removals. Remember that it is going to save a lot of work in the future if current breakages are held in place with adhesive tape until you can get around to making a permanent repair.

The one thing you can be certain about in these days of standardisation is that you will not be able to buy a length of moulding from a timber merchant or DIY shop to match the pattern you require, so you are going to have to fashion it yourself. Do not despair, this is not too difficult a task.

Fortunately, in most cases, only a few inches are required. The first thing to do is prepare the broken area by making all the edges square and clean. If a section of beading has been shattered or broken off, make a diagonal cut with a small hand-saw right through the moulding, taking care not to cut into the carcase. Clean the area thoroughly with a chisel, making sure that all the old glue is removed and the surface is absolutely flat.

If the damaged area is in the centre of the beading or a section of a radius (like a piece of the edge of a pie-crust table), make the aperture wedge-shaped, so that a new section will slide into place until it makes, a tight fit without any suspicion of a gap.

Do not make any attempt to shape the piece used for the repair before gluing it into place; just fit it to the surfaces that are going to be glued to make a perfect joint, leaving a generous overhang all round to be planed and filed down after fixing. Try to select a new piece from wood similar to the original moulding, with a similar grain running in the right direction.

After the glue is hard you can start to shape it. Many simple beadings can be finished with just a plane and sandpaper but for the more intricate ones you will need gouges and carving tools.

The small projecting beads applied round edges of drawer fronts in use throughout the eighteenth century are particularly prone to damage. Called 'cock beads', they are secured in channels cut into the sides and bottom of the drawers and across the full depth of the top edge. Because they stick out from the flat surface of the drawer front, they are very liable to damage and so are worthy of special mention.

Cocked beadings of various sizes are available from a few timber merchants, but are also very easy to make. Most timber yards will run off a few metres of rectangular wood of suitable dimensions. All you have to do is round the forward edge with sandpaper.

When replacing cock beads, first decide whether to replace the whole length or only part of it. In cases where the damage is extensive, it is better to replace the whole side, while small repairs can be spliced in. Cut out the broken section; corner replacements will need mitring (that is, ensuring that the angle is 45°) to fit. The

new section is secured with glue and veneer pins and smoothed
down with a block plane and sandpaper to make an invisible repair.

Cockbead repair

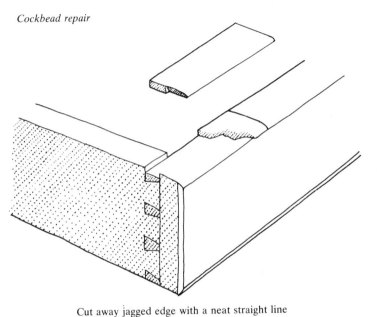

Cut away jagged edge with a neat straight line
and insert new piece

BEADS

When restringing beads, use a nylon thread rather than cotton and
tie a knot between each bead as future insurance against breaking.
Crystal beads in particular have sharp edges which can cut through
thread and in consequence are sometimes threaded on fine wire or
chain. If the holes through the beads are too small to take even the
finest needle, use very fine wire, such as thin fuse wire instead, as a

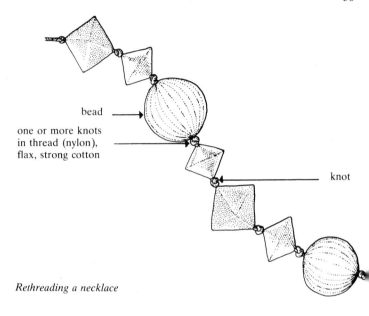

bead

one or more knots
in thread (nylon),
flax, strong cotton

knot

Rethreading a necklace

lead to pull the thread through. Alternatively, impregnate the end
of the thread with a quick-setting P.V.A. **adhesive** to stiffen it so
that it can be threaded through the bead more easily.

To repair broken glass beads or artificial stone ones, use Loctite
Glass Bond, now available from most ironmongers.

BEADWORK
The sewing of minute beads on to cloth backgrounds, to make
decorated articles such as fire screens and tea-cosies, was a pastime
for young Victorian ladies who had no radio or television to fill their
idle hours.

Carefully hand-wash in lukewarm water containing a detergent;
rinse in clean water and dry as quickly as possible with a hair dryer.

The majority of the beads used to form the patterns are so small
that you will have difficulty in finding a needle that will go through

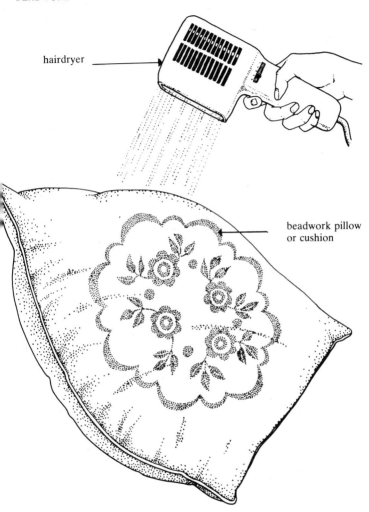

hairdryer

beadwork pillow
or cushion

How to dry beadwork

them. If repairs involve the replacing of beads, use a fine nylon fishing line, which is stiffer than cotton thread, only employing a needle after the bead has been threaded.

Beadwork can be ironed quite successfully by placing it face down on a padded ironing board and pressing the back.

BELLOWS
These normally have a wooden front and back, brass nozzle and leather sides. The valve is just a leather flap inside. If this wears out, the bellows have to be opened up and the flap replaced. The leather sides may also perish and need replacing. For normal leather treatments, see LEATHER.

BIRO STAINS – see BALLPOINT PEN STAINS

BISCUIT TINS – see TINWARE

BLOODSTAINS – see FABRICS, PAPER

BONE
It is not always easy to discriminate between bone and ivory. Bone is usually more coloured than ivory, and of a softer texture, and thus cannot be so deeply carved. It does not polish as well, and is more prone to have flaws and breaks in the surface.

The most valued bone objects are models, many made from mutton bone, by French prisoners during the Napoleonic Wars, but all kinds of animal bone have been used to make a wide variety of domestic objects, such as lace bobbins, salt spoons, paper knives etc. It has also been used widely for inlays in furniture and small articles such as tea caddies, particularly for key escutcheons and ornamental corners.

Cleaning is best carried out with a paste made with Whiting and Peroxide of Hydrogen. Make it to the consistency of toothpaste and apply liberally; allow to dry slowly. Sponge off the dry paste and polish with a clean duster or soft brush.

When carvings or other bone objects are cracked or otherwise damaged, preserve by immersion in molten candle wax for about five minutes. On removal, immediately wipe off any surplus wax and burnish with a duster.

Bone is quite easy to saw into flat pieces with a fine tooth saw, and these wafers can be cut into patterns for replacing missing portions of bone or ivory inlay with a jeweller's piercing or fret saw. Or fill missing areas with a white **filler** such as Brummer. If necessary, when dry, colour to match with a diluted **Woodstain**, or a matching shoe polish.

When bone objects have been broken they can be repaired with acrylic or Epoxy Resin **adhesives**. Epoxy Resin adhesives can also be used to fill in missing areas mixed to a paste with a filler such as French chalk and coloured with poster paint.

BOOKS

The greatest enemy of books is neglect. Unfortunately it is easy to put them away in a bookcase and forget that they are there. As with furniture, central heating can do great harm to books, as it leaches moisture from the atmosphere. Too dry an environment is as dangerous as one too humid.

Dust and damp are harmful – moulds, for instance, are induced by moisture – see **fungicides** for treatment. The other main enemies are bookworms, silverfish, book-boring beetles and firebrats. Some feed on the paper or the glue of the bindings, whilst some are attracted by the moulds.

The first rule in the care of books is to dust them regularly, even if they are kept in a closed bookcase; otherwise the dust which collects on the top of the pages will filter down and discolour the top margins. Even better than a duster is a small hand vacuum cleaner, as this will also collect any living pests that may lurk within.

Chemists supply moth-balls or Paradichlorobenzene crystals which will discourage nearly all insect pests, but bad infestations are difficult to eradicate totally. Fumigation appears to be the only satisfactory method, and professional aid should be sought. Modern insecticides are certainly effective, but as they are in either powder or liquid form, they are difficult to apply without marking or otherwise damaging the volumes.

Individual books can be disinfested by placing in an airtight box with Paradichlorobenzene crystals or some other fumigant for a day or so. More permanent protection can be provided by removing all the books from the bookcase and spraying the back and shelves with a long-lasting **insecticide** such as Lindane, which is the non-odorous variety of BHC.

For the removal of watermarks, fungus and mould damage, see PAPER. To treat stains, spotting and foxing, see PAPER.

The hard-back covers of books often become detached through rough handling and here a repair can be made by sticking together with a strip of 1in. Sellotape almost the same length as the pages. Leave a little play in the joint to allow for opening and closing.

Torn out or otherwise detached pages can be resecured in place with a strip of strong, acid free tissue or rice paper, using either white office paste, such as Gloy or one of the wallpaper pastes sold by decorators' shops.

Torn pages can also be repaired with the same pastes, carefully moistening the edges of the tear and pressing together with a sheet of rice paper or cigarette paper positioned on either side of the tear. This will absorb any surplus paste and prevent the pages sticking together. The majority of the backing sheets can be gently torn away, leaving parts adhering to the join. In most cases you will find that the text can be read through the thin layer of tissue.

Leather bindings also deteriorate over the years and should when necessary be given a clean-up with saddle soap to remove grime and light stains. Follow by a polish with British Museum Leather Dressing (see **leather treatments** for recipe.) An alternative which both cleans and preserves at the same time is sold under the trade name of Fortificuir.

Cloth bindings can often be brightened up with one of the proprietory spot-removing dry-cleaning fluids, applied with a soft duster just slightly damped with the liquid.

Bookbinding and repairing can be a fascinating hobby, and there are numerous reference books on the subject – try your public library.

Bookbinding supplies can be obtained from: Russell Bookcrafts*, or J. Hewitt & Sons*.

BOULLE

This extremely ornate tortoiseshell and brass inlaid furniture is named after a distinguished French ebonist, who popularised the style during the reign of Louis XV. He was not, however, the inventor of the process, as the use of tortoiseshell for the decoration of furniture, boxes and mirrors is recorded at least a hundred years earlier in Italy and around the Mediterranean.

Thin brass sheeting was fretted into intricate designs and applied to the body of the furniture. The intervening gaps were filled in with vari-coloured tortoiseshell.

Discoloured brass is extremely difficult to clean without scratching the tortoiseshell, and great care and patience is called for. It is best to use a paste made of fine pumice powder and vaseline mixed together. This preparation also feeds and polishes the tortoiseshell.

If only the tortoiseshell needs reviving, having gone dull and dead looking, the brilliance is restored by wiping over the surface with a damp, soapy rag, followed by a rinse with clean water, and drying. Next burnish vigorously with a chamois leather moistened with glycerine. This treatment will produce a lasting, brilliant polish – unless the shell has been exposed to full sunlight – in which case no amount of polishing will revive the dull texture.

Quite often you will find that sections of the brass inlay have become detached from the body of the furniture. They are often very springy and sometimes have been stretched or bent out of shape. The first essential task is to remove all the old glue, dirt, dust and grease completely. Next, the brass inlay must be made to fit. This may involve removing it, or even cutting the part that has become detached from the wooden surface away from the rest of the brass sheet that is still firmly glued down. Once detached, it can be hammered flat and if necessary filed down to fit the cavity before regluing it with Epoxy Resin **adhesive**.

To stick back loose pieces of tortoiseshell, use the same adhesive.

Where a piece is missing, fill small areas with a coloured hard wax **filler** (a type of sealing wax). A mixture of dark brown, red or yellow filler is best.

With practice, you will find that it is not very difficult to make imitation tortoiseshell if you melt the different colours of wax on the heated tang (the part that fits into the handle) of an old file, and dribble it into the cavity. It hardens in a few seconds and can be cut down flat to the surface with a sharp chisel.

BRASS AND COPPER

The cleaning of dulled brass and copper articles with a household metal polish is a simple chore that needs no explanation. What is not generally known is that the interval between cleaning sessions can be very considerably extended by polishing the cleaned brass with a good wax polish. The layer of burnished wax forms a skin over the metal which excludes the air and therefore inhibits oxidization. This treatment is far superior to the use of metal lacquers which – even the newest and best of them – leave a slightly detectable film that detracts from the deep sheen visible on newly burnished brass or copper.

The real problem with the cleaning of these metals arises when they have been neglected for long periods and have turned black, green, or a combination of the two.

The most effective *and* easy method, because the materials are always at hand, is to place kitchen salt on a half lemon and scour it over the metal's surface; alternatively, try soaking smaller items in a hot bath made up of a cup of vinegar and a heaped tablespoon of salt in a pint of boiling water. These treatments will remove all but the most persistent corrosion.

For this, use a non-caustic **paint stripper** such as Nitromors. Apply with a brush, leave for a few minutes, then wash off. A solution of Oxalic acid is also very effective. Use about two fluid ounces saturated solution and one heaped tablespoon of salt in a pint of water. After any of these treatments, wash thoroughly in clean water and then polish with one of the normal metal polishes. A final burnish with a duster and a mild abrasive such as Whiting (French chalk) or Tripoli powder will give the finest finish obtainable.

Clock repairers and Instrument makers use a chemical cleaner called Horolene. The concentrate is diluted as per the instructions and the articles are immersed in the solution for several hours.

An effective professional treatment for badly corroded objects is Cubrite which rapidly removes corrosion from copper and brass, rendering the surface either bright and glossy or receptive to surface coatings. Cubrite is manufactured by Jenolite Ltd and distributed by Frank W. Joel Ltd*.

See also **Metal cleaners**.

BRASS AND COPPER FITTINGS

Before attempting to clean any brass or copper fittings which are part of a piece of furniture, such as drawer handles or applied decorations (but not, of course, inlays or stringing), remove them. This is not a difficult operation; they are held in place only by screws or brass nails and attempts tó clean such metal parts *in situ* may damage the surrounding woodwork.

Inlays and stringing can be cleaned with metal polish rubbed on with a very fine grade of steel wool (grade 0000 or 000) see **abrasives**. This will remove any polish on the wooden part of the item in question, but it is likely that, if the inlays are in such bad condition, the woodwork also can do with renovation. When scouring brasswork which is set in wood, always rub steel wool in the direction of the grain, not across it to ensure no visible scratches are made on the wood's surface.

If you have a power-driven rotary polishing mop, your cleaning and polishing problems are reduced considerably. All you need is a calico polishing mop and a bar of suitable cleaning and polishing compound – see **Metal Polishes**. Alternatively, the Yellow Pages give the names of local Electro-platers or Metal Finishers, who may stock various compounds.

If they are not going to be used as household utensils, such as saucepans, repair broken articles with Epoxy Resin **adhesives**. In order to achieve a strong join, the two surfaces to be glued together must be thoroughly cleaned and de-greased. First use a fine file or sandpaper to brighten and roughen up the areas of contact, then apply methylated spirit 🔥 or other solvent and scrub with a small bristle brush. Now join, wait until completely set before tackling further renovation.

To repair holes, Epoxy Resins or Cyanoacrylate Ester **adhesives** (which will join all metals) can be used. The Epoxy Resin is mixed with a suitably coloured metallic powder (obtainable from an art shop) to a stiff paste and applied to the hole. It is usually necessary to make a back support to hold the metallic paste while drying and hardening takes place.

With small holes, one or two layers of Sellotape will suffice: with larger holes a more substantial backing will be required. When dry the repair can be rubbed down and lacquered before polishing with a **wax polish**.

Such repairs are suitable for display items only. Joints will have little durable strength. For durable repairs professional brazing or silver soldering is necessary.

BRASS AND TORTOISESHELL INLAY – see BOULLE

BRITANNIA METAL
This alloy was first used to fashion flatware and such items as teapots and drinking vessels in the last quarter of the eighteenth century. It is a mixture of antimony, copper, lead and tin in varying quantities and looks somewhat like pewter, but is much lighter and has a harder feel. So-called antimony boxes are often cast in Britannia metal.

As a variation on EPNS plated wares, you will often find it marked with EPBM (Electro Plated Britannia Metal). The metal is more brittle than either nickel silver or copper, which are both used as a base for silver plating, and it tends to fracture rather than dent if roughly handled.

Clean as for any other silver-plated article. When neglected, Britannia metal becomes dull grey and rubbing with mild abrasive powder, such as Jeweller's rouge or a patent silver cleaner will remove light corrosion. But remember that too harsh cleaning will remove silver plating as well.

Repairs are more difficult that with most other metals; soldering can be undertaken by an expert, following much the same rules as for repairing pewter. Replating also presents problems, but most electro-platers will undertake this work.

BRONZES

This is one of the oldest metals known to man, and articles
fashioned in this alloy are recorded as early as 2000 BC. It is
basically a mixture of copper and tin, in varying proportions for
different purposes. For instance, bell metal is 77% copper, 23% tin;
gun metal 90% copper, 10% tin. Statue bronze is an alloy of copper,
zinc, tin and lead.

When examining or buying bronzes, you have to make certain
that they are in fact bronze. From Victorian times a very large
number of statues and figures were cast in a base metal called
spelter and then 'bronzed' to look like the real article. More
recently extremely good copies of bronzes have been cast in plastic,
now produced to such a high standard that they can be and
sometimes are passed off as genuine to the unwary purchaser.

Spelter figures are easy to detect by nicking them with a penknife
in an unobtrusive place. The bright silver metal will show through
the bronze skin. Plastic pieces do not have the ring of true bronze,
but they may be just as heavy, as they are often weighted, either for
stability or sometimes to deceive.

Clean neglected bronzes by washing in lukewarm water and soap
(not detergent). The quality and value of bronzes largely depends
on the patina they have acquired, so great care must be taken to
preserve it. Never subject bronzes to steel wool or metal polishes or
you remove the patina – not even when there are green spots or
bubbles on the surface; they are caused by chlorine in the
atmosphere attacking the copper in the alloy. If the deterioration is
chronic, professional assistance must be sought, but minor damage
can often be treated successfully with a 10% solution of Acetic acid,
which you can obtain from the chemist. (Vinegar is a form of Acetic
acid, but it is not concentrated enough for this purpose.) Paint the
liquid on the affected areas and keep them damp to allow the acid to
get to work, scrubbing the surface with a soft brush. Under no
circumstances use steel wool or a wire brush, or you will remove the
patination.

Artificially induced patinas are applied to bronzes when they are
first made. These are either green or brown which, with age and
polishing, mellow into a deep glow indicating the quality of the

piece. Only an expert can restore such colourings chemically when the bronze has been damaged. You could try a coloured wax polish, to tint and blend in the damaged area with the rest of the article, but the experts will probably do it better! Mix shoe cream and polish together to obtain the correct hue; powdered poster colours can be mixed into the polish, instead of coloured shoe cream. Final polishing and protection of bronzes can be done with a good quality **wax polish** made of beeswax with the addition of about 5% of Carnauba wax. Most good quality antique furniture polishes are formulated in this way.

BUBBLING OF VENEER — see FURNITURE REPAIRS – VENEERS

BUTTON-BACK UPHOLSTERY
When buttons come off, you have to remove the back of the piece of furniture and sew the button back with strong string and a pad of hessian or similar material. There is a special long needle for this. It cannot be done from the front.

CALOTYPES
Do not attempt to clean or repair these yourself. Send to an expert.

CAMEOS
A cameo is produced when a shell or stone is carved to exploit the layers of differing colours which lie around and within the stone. The most common cameos are carved shells, usually having a cream or white raised portion carved into a portrait head, with a pink or red background. Various semi-precious stones have also been used to produce cameos, such as onyx and rock crystal. Ceramic cameos are also manufactured, the most famous by Wedgwood, inspired by the famous Portland Vase. Alas, today there are also plastic cameos on the market, some of them good enough to mislead at first sight.

Cameos should not be confused with intaglios, where the design is cut into the stone (as with seals), not as a raised relief carving. Many come from the Eastern Mediterranean and very early examples, dating back to the Roman Empire, can still be found in antique shops specialising in jewellery.

Resewing a button on to button-back upholstery

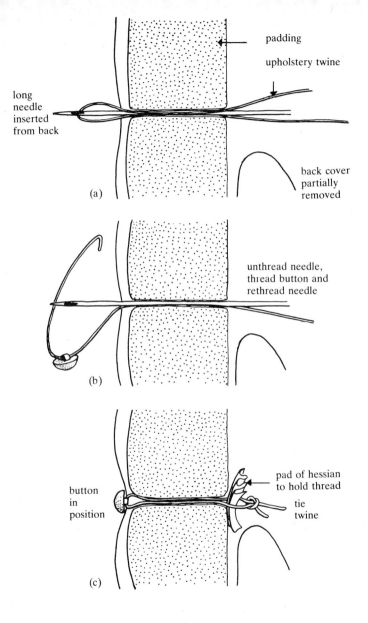

padding

upholstery twine

long needle inserted from back

back cover partially removed

(a)

unthread needle, thread button and rethread needle

(b)

button in position

pad of hessian to hold thread

tie twine

(c)

Cameos are simple to clean. The best and safest method is to scrub them with a nail brush in warm soapy water, then wash out thoroughly under a running tap to remove any soap residue. If the mounts are dull and have lost their sparkle, use Goddard's Jewellery Care.

Occasionally cameos get broken or chipped. Stick together with Cyanoacrylate Ester or Epoxy Resin **adhesives**. Care must be taken to keep the adhesive off the face of the cameo, particularly when bringing the two parts together, so apply the glue very thinly. To hold the parts while the adhesive is drying, make a 'jig' out of plasticine or modelling clay by holding the broken cameo parts together and pushing them into a ball made of putty or clay. Now glue the parts and replace the whole in the jig until completely set.

CAMERAS

Antique cameras are, today, eminently collectable, but are not used very much for taking photographs. On the other hand 'magic lanterns' are often used for entertainment as they provide the most convenient means of projecting old lantern slides.

The cleaning of photographic equipment of this kind is largely common sense. Cameras are a combination of the crafts of instrument-maker, cabinet-maker and leather craftsmen. Both woodwork and brass were often lacquered and, because the equipment was usually well looked after, the only deterioration normally experienced is the ravages of dust. Blow it away with a vacuum cleaner or brush away with a soft brush. Artists' sable paint brushes are best for dusting off lenses; clean with Kodak Lens Cleaner, obtainable from photographic dealers. This preparation can be used with confidence even on coated lenses.

To revive leather bellows and cases, use British Museum Leather Dressing (see **leather treatments** for recipe). If the black Morocco leather has been badly scuffed and shows grey, a coat of artist's Indian ink, applied with a water-colour brush, followed by leather dressing, will restore the finish.

Scratches in wooden bodies of cameras may call for repolishing, but this is the time to call on the services of an expert if you are not familiar with the technique. Where blemishes and scratches are

superficial, try a reviving agent such as Topp's Scratch Cover or
Furniglas No. 2.

CANEWORK

Caned panel-backed and seated chairs came into fashion in England
soon after the restoration of Charles II to the throne, and lasted all
through the high-back chair period, gradually becoming obsolete
from about 1700. It did not come into real vogue again until the
Regency, at the end of the eighteenth century.

As it grows older, canework gets darker and browner; when the
cane has to be replaced on antique furniture, it is usual to stain it so
that it does not look too new. The cane used is split rattan, which
has a shiny outer surface and repels many stains. Brush on a strong
concentration of analine walnut stain in methylated spirit; then wipe
off with an old rag to give the right effect.

Canework attracts dirt and dust which lodge in the meshes of the
weaving. Scrubbing with a stiff bristle brush and warm soapy water
will remove most superficial dirt, but ingrained grime may need
more determination. Try wetting the canework thoroughly with
warm water and then, with an old paintbrush, dab on white baking
powder, allow this to dry and brush off. Follow this treatment with a
thorough wash with cold water, and dry in the sun.

Sometimes you will encounter canework that has been 'protected'
by varnishing, and the varnish has darkened and started to flake off
in places. In such cases the whole of the old varnish has to be
removed. Some or, if you are lucky, all of this will come off when
rubbed over with coarse steel wool (see **abrasives**); if it does not, try
a **paint stripper**. But when applying the stripper, take great care to
ensure that it does not get on to the wooden frames, except where
the cane passes through the frame holes. As an added precaution,
use masking tape. Again wire wool will assist in the removal of the
offending varnish, but it is a messy job and rubber gloves are
advised. The last vestiges of varnish should be washed off with white
spirit, best applied with a soft rag. .

Broken strands can be repaired by sticking a bridging piece of
new cane at the back of the break, using one of the quick-drying
Acrylic **adhesives**. One in an easy-to-use tube with an extended

nozzle is the most convenient.

At one time recaning was work undertaken by the blind. There are very few specialists who undertake it these days, but you may find one in the Yellow Pages. Otherwise you will have to undertake the task yourself. You can obtain split rattan from handicraft shops, or direct from Dryad Handicrafts*.

CARPETS

Nearly all antique carpets come from Turkey, Persia, India or China. Not until the seventeenth century, when the French court encouraged the foundation of two carpet factories (the Louvre Gallery in 1605 and the Savonnerie in 1627) was an industry established in Europe. They were not made in England for nearly another century.

Carpets are distinguishable from tapestries because the threads are knotted, not woven. Modern European carpets do not have knots, the pile being held by the weave of the backing canvas. Thus, when buying antique carpets, you must ensure that they are hand-knotted and not machine-woven. The quality of a carpet depends to a great extent on the number of knots to the square inch: the more knots, the better the carpet.

Having established that it is hand-made, examine it carefully at the back for thin patches by holding it up to the light. Weak areas, repairs and holes will be easily seen. Variations in colour and shape (carpets are sometimes out of square) should not be considered as detracting from their value. Most carpets were made by nomadic tribeswomen who had to dismantle and set up their looms many times during the manufacture of any one carpet. The wool would not all have been dyed at one time, and distortion of the shape might also have taken place during the frequent moves. These imperfections are admired rather than considered cause for criticism.

Several kinds of knots will be found in hand-made carpets, but it is difficult for a non-expert to distinguish between them. The golden rule, as always when in doubt, is to consult an expert. Some rugs and carpets are extremely valuable, particularly very old 'Persian' ones. Today carpets and rugs are almost invariably used as floor

Carpets

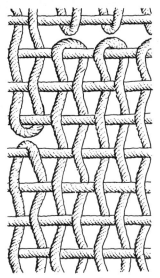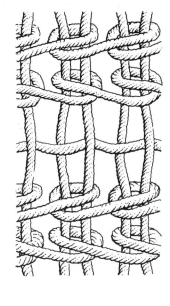

(a) different types of weaves

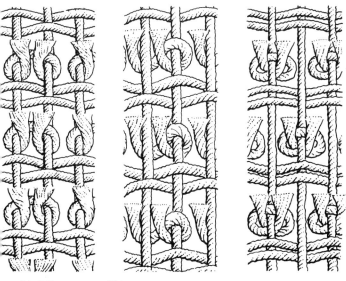

(b) different types of knots

coverings. This means that they get extremely hard wear and tear and are subjected to sharp grit which gets ground into the pile and can cause damage, as well as making the rug dull and shabby. In earlier times, certainly up to the seventeenth century, carpets and rugs were only used as table coverings and wall hangings, the floor being strewn with rushes.

For day-to-day cleaning, there is no better method than thorough vacuuming. Where possible, turn back larger rugs and carpets and vacuum-clean the back before the front. Dust and grit tend to filter through to the floor, so remove this with suction before vacuuming the pile side. On no account take an old or valuable rug and shake it while holding on to one end or the side: this subjects the warp of the article to excessive strain and could cause serious damage. You can tap the carpet very gently after draping it over a line – but do not beat.

Before washing or shampooing an old carpet, make a test to find out if the colours are really fast. Thoroughly wet and rub between the hands a small section, and then rub the wetted area with a clean dry white cloth. If there is any transferral of dye, consult an expert.

The traditional method of cleaning badly grimed carpets is washing with yellow soap and water, but this is not a very practical solution for the average collector. There are, however, several methods that can be carried out at home. All-over cleaning with one of the proprietary carpet cleaners, obtainable from any hardware shop, is much easier if you hire or borrow a shampooing machine which applies the correct amount of cleaning fluid, rubs it in, and then removes the surplus moisture and dirt by suction. Consult the Yellow Pages for such a machine.

Another alternative is steam cleaning, carried out by on-site contractors who will do the job for you at home. In some areas you can also hire the machines by the day from tool-hire shops. Again, try the Yellow Pages. These machines apply small quantities of hot water mixed with a detergent under pressure right into the carpet and immediately after suck up the grimy moisture into a container. Until the slightly damp carpet has thoroughly dried, do not replace any furniture, as the weight will make indentations that will be difficult to remove.

Localised soiling of carpets should be treated immediately; tackle grease spots with **Fuller's earth** or French chalk. Dust the powder all over the affected area and leave for twenty-four hours; brush away and then vacuum-clean. Sometimes the nature of the grease is such that you will have to resort to a **solvent**.

Simple repairs, such as frayed edges, tattered fringes, can also be tackled without recourse to specialist help. A stout needle and some strong matching thread is all that is required to prevent fraying.

CAST IRON – see IRON and **Rust removers**

CASTORS – see under FURNITURE REPAIRS

CERAMICS
All ceramics are made of various types of clay, are fired in a kiln, and have a glazed surface. Earthenware is the most widely used, and is opaque and less robust than other forms of ceramic. If the glazed surface becomes chipped or cracked, water and stains penetrate and discolour the porous body. It is made from various types of china clay, fired at a relatively low temperature, and was traditionally used for the manufacture of ornaments and domestic utensils. Bone china was invented by Josiah Spode in the late eighteenth century, who introduced bone ash into a mixture of kaolin and Cornish stone (felspar) to produce a finer, translucent and altogether more attractive ceramic than earthenware. Porcelain has no bone ash, but contains felspar, quartz and lime which give it an extremely delicate feel. It is even harder than bone china.

Stoneware is a material much favoured by modern studio potters, and is similar to porcelain in terms of hardness. Common stoneware has a basis of fine clay and various silicates. It contains similar ingredients to porcelain and is heat resistant.

As most colours will not survive firing at the extremely high temperatures needed to produce porcelain and bone china, they are often applied after the glaze has been fired. This means that when cleaning badly stained articles, care must be taken, particularly with gold embellishments, not to damage or rub off the decoration. As a general rule, all types of ceramics only require washing in warm water containing some household detergent. Avoid the use of abrasive materials (including nylon brushes and swabs) on old or delicate articles when washing. Use a plastic bowl to guard against breakage.

After washing, rinsing and drying, the lustre is improved by gentle polishing with a soft, dry chamois leather. Valuable antique ceramics should not even be washed just dusted with a sable brush.

Badly stained pieces, such as teapots can sometimes be cleaned by the application of **bleaching agents**. First try 20 volumes Peroxide of Hydrogen. Household and industrial bleaches can be tried, but there is a danger of damage to the decoration. Proprietary stain removers, available from most Boots branches and chemists are sold under the names of Chempro T and Stainfree. For the inside of narrow-necked vessels, where a brush cannot easily be inserted, use Steradent denture cleaner.

Broken and chipped china can be repaired, using either Acrylic or Epoxy Resin **adhesives**. The newer Cyanoacrylate Ester **adhesives** are also excellent, but expensive. The technique is to use as little glue as possible after ensuring that the pieces are free from all dirt and grease, fit perfectly and after gluing can be held firmly in place while hardening.

If you are going to undertake ceramic repairs, work with a magnifying glass on a flexible stand. Old repairs, badly executed with either animal or cellulose glues can be released by soaking in hot water or baking in a low oven for 20–30 minutes. Every last particle of the old adhesive and any dirt must now be removed and the parts brought together to prove a perfect fit.

Next construct a 'cradle' or holding device in which to rest the joined pieces until the joint has hardened. A number of devices can be employed, the most practical and easy being plasticine, a box containing dry silver sand, and self-adhesive tape. Having prepared your resting place, a very very thin coat of adhesive should be applied to both surfaces and any surplus that is squeezed out removed with **solvent** on a piece of rag. A slight damping with methylated spirit will do.

With chips, or when pieces are missing, they can be modelled in with an Epoxy Resin putty **filler** called Sylmasta, available from most artists' suppliers. Make the new part slightly thicker than the rest of the body, so that when it is dry it can be rubbed down to match exactly with fine garnet or wet-and-dry paper (see **abrasives**).

Colouring in any missing design is best done with acrylic paints, available from any art shop. When dry (and they dry quite quickly) they can be glazed with a clear Polyurethane **lacquer**.

These are only the bare first principles of china restoring. One of the best books on the subject is *Mending and Restoring China* by Thomas Pond (London, Garnstone Press).

CHAIN
The best way to clean this is to use a tumbler; otherwise use a wire brush.

CHAIN MAIL
Clean as ordinary steel.

CHAIN PURSES
Clean with a silver brush or similar.

CHAIR LEGS – see under FURNITURE REPAIRS

CHAMPLEVE – see ENAMELLED WARE

CHANDELIERS
Chandeliers are most commonly assemblies of crystal glass beads, cut in such a way that they reflect the maximum amount of light. The original light source was of course candles, now superseded by electric bulbs imitating candles. Sometimes the crystal beads and drops are supported on a brass or other metal frame, often the whole chandelier is made of glass elements. Other materials, such as ceramics, brass and other metals are also used in their making.

Fixed to the ceiling, they are exposed to the maximum of smoke, dust and other floating débris, and fairly quickly lose their sparkle and thus need regular cleaning. This is best done at ground level and, as large chandeliers are very heavy, it is sensible to install them on some kind of pulley system.

Chandeliers can always be dismantled into their separate elements; they are only held together by wire, usually brass or some other non-ferous metal. Wash them in warm water containing some Scrubb's ammonia, detergent, or both. Dry each segment thoroughly with a soft cloth or chamois leather. The traditional way to keep them bright in the days when candles were burnt was to rub over each lustre wearing a pair of chamois gloves.

Cleaning over a long period of time causes metal fatigue and failure in some of the wire ties; keep an eye on the latter as they will have to be replaced from time to time. This is easy, as each drop and bead has one or two holes for joining purposes. Do not use steel wire for replacement, as this will eventually rust and stain the crystals. Replace broken or missing elements. Your local antique dealer or lighting shop may be able to help with spare lustres; if not, you will usually find what you want at Christopher Wray's Lighting Emporium* in London.

See also GLASS.

CHINA – see CERAMICS

CHINA DOLLS – see DOLLS

CLOCKS

The amount of cleaning and renovation of clocks that you undertake depends on two things: the value of the clock and how expert you are with delicate machinery. In this section only the 'works' are dealt with. For the conservation of clock cases, refer to the FURNITURE section.

Clocks dating back to the fifteenth and sixteenth centuries are very rare, while eighteenth-century clocks are valuable and much collected. Antique clocks fall into two main categories: those driven by weights and those driven by a spring. Both types may have a pendulum to regulate the time, but many mantel and bracket clocks rely on a regulator. Many mantel clocks have a special screw for securing the pendulum when the clock has to be moved. Examination of the back will reveal what steps you need to take to avoid damage during transportation.

Grandfather/longcase clocks

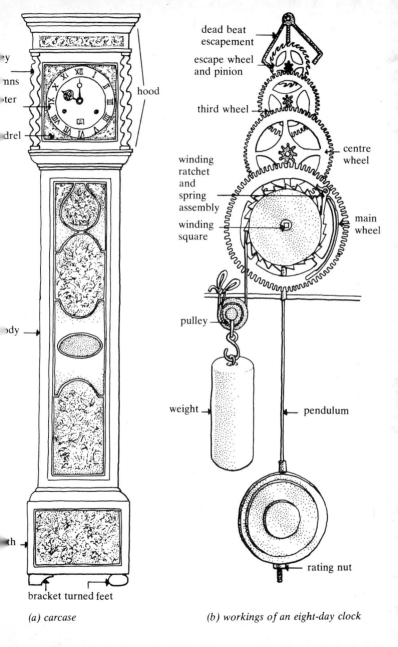

dead beat
escapement

escape wheel
and pinion

third wheel

centre
wheel

winding
ratchet
and
spring
assembly

winding
square

main
wheel

pulley

weight

pendulum

rating nut

(b) workings of an eight-day clock

·y

nns

·ter

·drel

hood

·dy

·th

bracket turned feet

(a) carcase

The grandfather or long-case clock is the best known of the pendulum clocks. Most were built in the eighteenth and nineteenth centuries and the basic mechanism is very simple and robust. Cottage clocks go for thirty hours on a winding, better ones for eight days. The long case contains either one or two weights, one to operate the hands, one the striking mechanism. The mechanism is revealed when the hood is removed; usually by sliding the top section containing the glass door forward but sometimes, in earlier clocks, by lifting the hood towards the ceiling.

The main purpose of the hood is to protect the movement from dust, for it is this above all else that causes damage and thus erratic time-keeping. Dust combines with the lubricating oil on the moving parts to make an abrasive paste that wears away the bearings and pinions. Together with damp, which can cause corrosion, these are the clock's great enemies. Always use a spirit level when placing a clock in position. Some will not function at all if they are not properly levelled, but all clocks should have a properly prepared resting place. With long-case clocks it is advisable to secure them to the wall to avoid accidents. This also ensures that when floors are being polished the clock is not moved.

The pendulum

When setting a pendulum clock in motion, you can hear from the tick if it is standing properly: if the clock does not have a nice, even beat, it is not standing level. Pendulum clocks are regulated by lengthening or shortening the pendulum by means of a screw below and securing the weight. This can be tightened (shortening the pendulum) to make the clocks go faster and vice versa. When moving a long-case clock, always dismount the pendulum by carefully unhooking it. If you look behind the works, you will see that the top of the pendulum rod is joined to a length of flat spring with a block of metal fixed to the other end. This is hung in a slit, in such a way that the pendulum swings back and forth between the prongs of a fork, which in turn controls the claw-like 'escapement'. This has to be carefully unhooked as the length of spring called 'the feather' is easily damaged. The weights also have to be unhooked. When this is done, the movement, complete with the face, can normally be removed from the case.

The striking mechanism

If this gets out of step with the hands, it usually means that the striking plate, a large brass disc with slots in it, has slipped. This is corrected by releasing (usually lifting) the finger lodged in one of the slots, allowing the clock to strike. Repeat the process until chime and hands are in agreement.

Winding

Clocks like to be wound regularly. This helps them to keep good time. When winding a thirty-hour clock by pulling up the weight by rope or chain, support the weight with your free hand, as it helps to reduce wear. When winding key-wound clocks, do so evenly, counting the number of turns to avoid winding the spring so tight that it cannot go any further.

Removing dust

From time to time blow dust out of the works of a clock with a hair dryer or by reversing the hose on a vacuum cleaner.

Oiling

Cleaning and oiling a clock is a specialist's job, and should be done about every five years. If you want to oil a clock yourself, use the correct kind of oil (obtainable from a clock repairer). On no account use ordinary lubricating oil, and only oil the bearings: do not put any oil on the gears.

CLOISONNE – see ENAMELLED WARE

COCK BEADS – see BEADING AND STRINGING

COFFEE STAINS – see FABRICS, PAPER

COINS

Whether or not you clean coins depends on what you are going to do with them. If you are a coin collector, you will know that the rule is *don't clean* them, as cleaning drastically reduces their value. Indeed, if the coins are in mint, or near mint condition, you only handle them by grasping the edges.

If, on the other hand, you are going to use some coins of little value for decorative purposes, such as bracelets, pendants, a coffee table surface or a wall plaque, by all means shine them up.

Gold coins do not tarnish, so just wash them in warm water and dry them on a soft washleather. Silver coins can be brightened up with Goddard's Silver Dip, or rubbing them gently with cotton wool impregnated with a **solvent** Carbon Tetrachloride, and then immediately washed and dried. Old copper coins can be dipped for a few seconds only into a 5% to 10% solution of Nitric acid before immediate removal to a basin of water. Too long exposure to the acid will etch the surface, so great care must be taken. You can also use Silver Dip on copper coins, and it has much the same effect.

If you find ancient coins which have been buried or otherwise hidden, take them to your nearest museum without attempting to clean them in any way. The curator will tell you what to do with them and give you professional help.

To keep coins bright, polish them with a **wax polish**, or Goddard's Long Term Silver Polish. This will retard tarnishing for long periods.

COPPER – see BRASS and COPPER

CORAL
Coral is the skeleton or shell of small animals which inhabit the sea, and is basically limestone. The best coral is found in the Mediterranean Sea and is a delicate pink in colour. There are still coral fishing and manufacturing industries in Italy and North Africa. Coral jewellery has been made for centuries and every few years enjoys a fresh vogue of popularity, but it is the beautifully carved *objets de vertu* which are the most collectable items.

Clean coral pieces by washing thoroughly in warm soapy water and scrub with a tooth- or nail-brush to remove lingering dirt from inaccessible cracks.

If coral comes in contact with acids, the surface will lose some of its smoothness and attractive polish. This can be restored by burnishing the affected areas with a mild **abrasive**, such as Jeweller's rouge or fine Pumice powder. To rejoin broken pieces, use

Cyanoacrylate Ester or Epoxy Resin **adhesives**. When trying to join very small pieces together with glue, there are certain preparations that should be taken to make the task as easy as possible and avoid frustration. First, use a pair of dissecting or other long, fine tweezers to avoid getting glue on your fingers and prevent the work being obscured. Second, devise a simple 'jig' to hold the pieces. A ball of plasticine is one of the most useful tools for this purpose. Finally, once the pieces are correctly placed together, lay them aside without disturbance to stick properly; in this way you will achieve a firm repair.

CRACKS – see CERAMICS, FURNITURE REPAIRS and **adhesives**

DAGGERS – see WEAPONS

DAGUERROTYPES
Do not touch.

DAMP – see PAPER, FURNITURE REPAIRS – DAMAGE THROUGH DAMP

DIAMONDS – see JEWELLERY

DISCOLORATION – see under item and also **bleaching agents, colouring agents** and **solvents**

DOLLS
Dolls, over the years, have been made from a considerable variety of materials and many are a composite of several different elements. For instance, dolls with ceramic heads and arms and cloth bodies are quite common, as are those made of bisque or Parian-ware.
    Ceramic dolls were usually made of glazed china or porcelain, bisque (unglazed porcelain) or occasionally Parian-ware (unglazed white clay imitating marble).

China dolls
The heads of china dolls are almost always modelled complete with shoulders into which a number of holes have been made for

attachment to the body.

Highly glazed china dolls are quite easily cleaned. First, discoloured glue should be removed by gently brushing with an old tooth- or nail-brush, after soaking. In extreme cases add a tablespoon of ammonia or bleach to a pint of water, which may help to shift the glue. Wash with household detergent in warm water.

Many nineteenth-century dolls have dark hair painted on the head; others have real hair attached. If the latter, take care when washing the china head, as the hair can be spoilt by wetting (see DOLLS' HAIR below). In cases where the doll is really dirty, you have to detach the hair for thorough cleaning. When heads are badly cracked, take care when making repairs, as these must be as invisible as possible. To make invisible joins, use P.V.A. or Cyanoacrylate Ester **adhesives**. Sometimes a rearrangement of the hair also helps in concealing bad breaks. If large pieces of the head are missing, first stick a piece of card or buckram to the inside of the head, then use a **filler** such as Sylmasta.

Bisque and Parian-ware dolls
Being unglazed, the surfaces absorb dirt and grease over the years. This makes cleaning a little more difficult, particularly as the flesh and other colours are often painted on and will come off or run with washing. Choose an unobtrusive area and test before jumping in with both feet! Using a tooth-brush, work over the surface with Scrubb's household ammonia or warm water containing washing-up liquid. If any persistent stains remain, use a fine Pumice stone very, very gently. Restore colouring by tinting with water-colour paints. When dry, protect the head with a light coating of clear wax polish.

Composition and papier mâché dolls
Sometimes complete dolls are made of composition; more often they are fitted with ceramic heads. Papier mâché dolls are made of compressed paper pulp mixed with glue and fillers, such as china clay. Both kinds are invariably painted, so proceed with caution when cleaning. Wipe over with a wad of cotton-wool lightly impregnated with white spirit and then swab lightly with warm soapy water. The ravages of time may have caused the paint to chip

or rub off. For both partial and complete repaints, use acrylic colours. To achieve flesh tones, mix white with cadmium red, yellow ochre and a touch of black. With a little experimentation, you can achieve a life-like hue. The recommended colours dry to a matt finish, but you may want a gloss finish. Any quick-drying varnish from an art shop is suitable; you will need two or three coats, finishing with at least one over the entire surface of the head.

Celluloid dolls
These are dangerous in the hands of young children, being highly inflammable. Celluloid was first used for doll manufacture in the 1880s. The material is usually quite thin and dents easily. Dents can sometimes be removed by soaking in hot water and sucking out. Failing this, stick a pin through the celluloid and try to pull it back into shape.

Plastic dolls
Not until the 1920s were plastics used for making dolls, and colours were often far from fast. To restore colour, use acrylic colours, which are also plastic, and thus will adhere and combine – unlike other paints – with the plastic body. Another frequently found fault is seams and joints splitting open. To repair, use plastic P.V.A. **adhesives**.

Wax dolls
These are among the earliest, most beautiful and most valuable to be found. They are also the most easily damaged, as wax is easily chipped or rubbed – and is softened by moderate heat. Remove surface dirt with cosmetic cleansing cream on a pad of cotton-wool. More deep-seated discoloration should be treated in the same way with real turpentine. You will be removing a layer of wax, so great care must be exercised to ensure that not too much of the wax is dissolved, otherwise all the colour will be removed. If you have a dolls' hospital in your area, first seek their advice or try to find a dealer who specialises in dolls. A new body, and the full range of limbs, eyes, etc., are available by post from Pollock's Toy Museum* in London.

Wooden dolls
These are usually very crudely made and are often of great
antiquity. With luck they have acquired an attractive patination and
will only be reduced in value by excessive cleaning. Consult an
expert before doing anything other than superficial cleaning with a
soft brush or damp cloth. If the damage is so great that repair is
essential, treat as for *Composition dolls* above. Lacquer if a gloss
finish is wanted. Joints are of the mortice and tenon variety, secured
with a metal pin, which often breaks. To repair, either glue them
back together or, if the damage is more severe, splice in a similar
piece of new wood.

DOLLS' BODIES
Dolls' bodies, like heads, are made of various materials. As far as
simple renovation is concerned, however, those made of cloth,
leather, or several rigid parts held together by elastic are the most
important.

Composition bodies are made from mixtures of all kinds of simple
materials, such as sawdust and glue, plaster, gesso, clay or bran. In
all cases, repair breaks with quick-drying P.V.A. **adhesives**. Cracks,
holes and missing portions can be modelled in with Polyfilla or
Epoxy Resin fillers such as Plastic Padding or Sylmasta, as can
missing hands, fingers, or feet. In order to ensure that larger pieces
are well attached to the stumps, it is best to dowel them on. That is,
insert a short length of wooden or metal dowel into the remaining
part of the limb, allowing it to extend as far as possible. Either drill a
hole to hold it or, if the limb is hollow, embed it in Sylmasta. Then
model the rest of the limb from the same material, using the dowel
as a rigid base.

Stuffed bodies often have china or composition hands and feet
sewn to the ends of arms and legs. The rest of the body is usually
made of stout cloth or soft leather. Most repairs consist of sewing
and patching, but on occasion more stuffing may have to be
introduced. In these cases try to match the texture of the original
filling material (if sawdust, use sawdust, etc.). Segmented bodies
often suffer from perished elastic, which is best replaced by a special
round elastic (available from the Altrincham Rubber Co.*). The

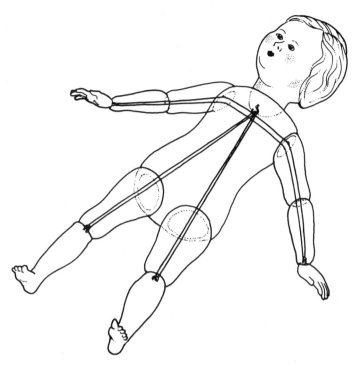

How doll's limbs are strung

extremity of each limb is fitted with a hook or loop. Pass one double length of elastic up each arm and across the shoulders, and a second double length up the legs and body to the neck. Both these cords holding the limbs together now hook on to the bottom of the doll's head. First make a bodkin-like tool from a piece of fairly rigid wire to facilitate the threading of the limbs together; second, to achieve the right degree of tension when knotting all the elastic ends at the neck hole, leave a few inches of elastic spare, so that you can adjust the knots until you get it right.

DOLLS' CLOTHES

If original clothes have survived, no matter how tatty the condition, their resurrection is essential if the value of the doll is to be enhanced. But for the adult collector, dressing antique dolls provides much of the attraction of the hobby. The correct period is important and reference to contemporary fashion plates or pattern books will provide you with the necessary guidance.

The refurbishing of the original garments calls for care and patience; outer garments are often loaded with the grime of ages. Do not think that you can get away with tossing them in the washing machine – old fabrics tend to be extremely fragile and should be cleaned with great care. First it is important to remove the major stains. Identification of the cause of stain can be difficult, but they normally fall into the following categories: 1. Grease and oil. 2. Ink. 3. Moulds. 4. Paint. 5. Rust. For detailed instructions on stain removal, see FABRICS.

Washing dolls' clothes obviously calls for a high degree of care. All coloured clothes have to be tried to make sure that the colours are fast. Washing should be by hand, and the normal rules of washing apply. Where white underclothes have become dingy, a final rinse in a weak peroxide of hydrogen solution will bleach back to white again. Where suitable, a light starching before careful ironing is a good idea. Never wash in very hot water and, if fabrics are fragile, do not wash at all but remove as much dirt as possible with **Fuller's earth** or warm bran. When in doubt, have the garments dry-cleaned. This applies particularly to brocades, watered silks, ring velvet, and non-fast coloured materials.

DOLLS' EYES

Before 1870, dolls were made with fixed eyes, either painted or of glass. 'Sleeping' dolls with counter-balanced eyes were not invented until after that date. Pairs of glass eyes, wired together, are held in place in plaster sockets. A lead weight on a short rigid wire is attached to the connecting wire at right angles and, as the doll is lowered to its back, or sat up, the weight opens or closes the eyes. Most china or bisque dolls' heads have a large hole in the top, which provides access for adjusting or repairing the eye mechanism,

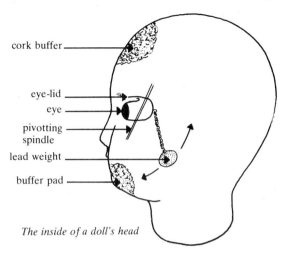

cork buffer

eye-lid

eye

pivotting
spindle

lead weight

buffer pad

The inside of a doll's head

covered by a cardboard or composition dome, in turn concealed by
the hair piece.

Partly to prevent scratching and as a lubricant, eyes were dipped
into melted wax. This wax was also used to fix the eyelashes in
place. The easiest way to replace eyelashes is to buy false ones from
a beauty shop and trim them down to size. Stick them on with the
eyeballs in place, to help get them properly positioned. (Use P.V.A.
glue, as cosmetic eyelash glue is not appropriate.)

DOLLS' HAIR

This was fixed by anything from one hank glued into a slit in the top
of the head, to a wig, glued on to a removable dome of strawboard
or composition, and is often tangled, matted and dirty. All kinds of
animal and synthetic hairs have traditionally been used. Should the
hair need replacing, try to obtain human hair, which is undoubtedly
the best and easiest to handle, though wig-maker's hair is the easiest
to obtain.

The first task is to untangle the hair; for this you need plenty of
patience, taking very little at a time, starting at the ends, not the

scalp, and trying not to pull out or break too many hairs. It can be washed, but dry shampooing with light magnesium carbonate or the proprietary dry shampoos for domestic animals, is easier and almost as effective. Alternatively, an application of heated bran will remove dirt. Just apply to the hair, work in with the finger tips, leave for five minutes or so, and then brush out.

Throughout the years, doll manufacturers have been slavish followers of hair fashion, so it is important to dress the hair as near to the fashion of the period at its time of manufacture as possible. Again, reference to suitable works on the subject is called for.

DOLLS' HOUSES

The decision that every owner of an antique dolls' house has to make is whether it is an adult's or a child's toy. When they are in reasonable condition, antique dolls' houses are of considerable value and have great charm. It is beyond the comprehension of small children that such an item has to be preserved in its original condition: they will inevitably want to spring-clean or decorate it, and such treatment may have dire consequences.

Far better, therefore, to give a child a new dolls' house to use as a toy and keep great-grandma's until maturity brings an appreciation of Victorian, or even Georgian miniature houses. Such houses, although designed originally as children's playthings, provide a great opportunity for an adult hobby. Renovating and restoring them is only a start: furnishing and stocking them can provide endless pleasure and an outlet for talent that the construction of anything miniature always brings.

If you are lucky enough to possess or to acquire an old dolls' house, first decide how much restoration you are going to do. As with antique furniture, patina, the charm of age, must not be destroyed. Do nothing without considering the final effect. Never repaint where you can clean. Never remove fittings, like wall and floor coverings, until you have found a suitable replacement. Of course, where parts are missing, replace them and finish to blend in with the fabric of the house. Loose or damaged parts should be glued back together again, and any visible signs of the repairs carefully concealed by touching up with matching paint or whatever finish is appropriate.

Very often dust and grime have become ingrained while a dolls' house has stood in an attic or store cupboard. Remove the superficial dirt, then tenacious grime can be carefully washed away with a household detergent, like Flash. Only attempt to clean a small area at a time, drying it carefully before moving on. Occasionally the brickwork, tiles, etc. are printed on paper stuck on the surface of the house, so take care not to soak them off.

You may encounter failure of glue joints due to perishing of the glue. Before regluing it is essential to clean off all the old, perished glue. Mend the joint with any Acrylic or P.V.A. **adhesive**.

Woodworm is sometimes encountered, particularly when plywood has been used in construction. This pest need no longer be feared, as modern proprietary woodworm killers (see **insecticides**) are totally effective if applied according to instructions. Damaged parts need only be replaced if they are beyond restoration. Fill the holes made by woodworm and other causes with a **filler** – such as Polyfilla.

Paintwork, over a long period of years, will have acquired that delightfully faded and mellow look that denotes age, and is so hard to simulate. Finishes of this kind should be disturbed as little as possible, and should never be over-cleaned. When repainting or retouching is unavoidable, use carefully matched poster paints. They are opaque, and fill up cracks if applied thickly. Slightly dilute and apply with a small flat brush, then brush out to give a smooth finish. If you require a gloss finish, use one coat of clear varnish such as Furniglas P.U.15. Use enamel paints only where a very high gloss is called for.

Interior decorating calls for the use of imagination and flair. For instance, hand paint wallpapers to simulate period designs in miniature, or use wrapping papers with small designs on them. Cut up illustrations in glossy magazines to provide floor coverings: indeed, there is no end to the ingenuity that can produce scaled-down artefacts.

The scale of most dolls' houses in Victorian times was 1 inch to the foot, but other reductions were also used, so watch this when either making or purchasing furnishings. You can often pick up miniature furniture, china-ware and household items in antique shops.

If you want to make your own dolls' house furniture, read *Furnishing Dolls' Houses* by Audrey Johnson (G. Bell & Son); Dover Books* (London and New York) also publish books containing cut-out dolls' house wallpapers and floor coverings.

You will find all kinds of dolls' house accessories in London at Pollock's Toy Museum.*

DRAWER RUNNERS – see under FURNITURE REPAIRS

DRAWER STOPS – see under FURNITURE REPAIRS

EGGSTAINS – see FABRICS, PAPER

EMBROIDERY

This is distinguished from tapestry by the fact that it is worked on to a piece of base material, whereas tapestry is woven into the base on a loom.

Secure the piece firmly to a frame before cleaning; otherwise, where the stitches are all in one direction, the piece may distort so badly that the original shape cannot be regained. Where embroidered furniture is concerned, there is great danger of shrinking, so it is better to try cleaning it without removing it from the piece of furniture. It can be cleaned *in situ* using Carbon Tetrachloride, see **solvents**. Where staining persists and the embroidery is standing up to treatment, try using a carpet shampoo.

Consult an expert before you touch old and valuable work.

On clothing, uniforms and regalia, metal filaments were frequently used as an embroidery thread. In time they become tarnished, but again, before attempting to clean it, consult an expert.

For further advice on cleaning fabrics see FABRICS.

ENAMELLED WARE

Enamel is produced by coating metal sheeting with a paste made from powdered glass mixed with suitable colouring materials and firing in a kiln. Several techniques have been employed over the years to keep the various colours from running together when the glass melts.

Different types of enamelling

(a) Cloisonné

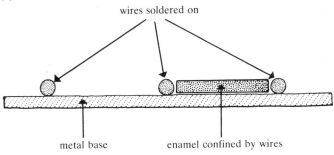

(b) Champlevé

Enamelling techniques were known to the ancient Egyptians and Greeks. Vast quantities of oriental enamel work were imported into the west, while many European jewellers, from Fabergé down, have used this highly durable, glossy form of decoration to embellish their products.

Cloisonné is usually in the form of vases or ornaments, the colours being separated by fine wires previously fixed to the metal base. Champlevé is produced by engraving the metal base and filling the hollows with different coloured pastes. Between 1750 and 1840, large quantities of small boxes and other small containers were produced in England by first firing a neutral base of enamel to the artefact and then painting with enamels, either freehand, or over transfers, and then firing for a second time. Battersea, Bilston and Birmingham were the main centres of the industry in England.

Because metal objects, unlike ceramics, do not break when they are dropped, much damaged enamelware is to be found. Obviously the value of such pieces is only a fraction of the perfect examples.

First, examine the piece to detect any previous restoration and ensure by trial that the repair is waterproof. As a general rule, clean with yellow soap and warm water. Where enamelling is only part of the object, and cannot be removed, or where water could cause damage, use a cleaning **solvent** such as acetone or Carbon Tetrachloride. Sometimes, even after cleaning, stains still remain in cracks: bleach these out with a **bleaching agent** such as Hydrogen Peroxide. Where parts of the enamel have broken away from the base, the only possible restoration that can be made is with paints of one kind or another, as refiring is out of the question. The Acrylic paints are certainly the easiest to use, having enough body to make up to the right thickness.

After painting in, and to consolidate any areas where flaking or lifting of the enamel is taking place, using an artists's sable watercolour brush, apply a thin coat of Polyurethane **lacquer** such as Furniglas P.U.15, though making sure that as much as possible is worked in under the flaking areas; when it is half-dry, very carefully wipe over the surface with a pad of cotton wool dampened (not soaked) with a mixture of white spirit mixed 3 parts to 1 with either cellulose thinners 🔥 or Xylene 🔥 (see **solvents**) to remove surplus adhesive residues which will spoil the surface if they are allowed to dry hard.

EPNS – see NICKEL SILVER

FABRICS
When cleaning fabrics of any kind, the following factors have to be taken into consideration.

1. Are the colours fast? Sometimes some of the colours are, but

others will run. Test fastness by wetting an unobtrusive section of the fabric and pressing it between sheets of white blotting paper. Traces of colour mean that the material, or some part of it, is not suitable for washing. Is the design painted or printed? Will it stand up to the proposed cleaning method? Painted fabrics, in particular, can be damaged by dry cleaners. Again, test first.

2. How fragile is the fabric? All natural fibres tend to deteriorate with age, and any chemical treatment may hasten the disintegration of a cherished heirloom. Many modern detergents contain bleaches and other ingredients which, though entirely suitable for modern clothes, are likely to harm fragile fabrics of great age. Always support such items by tacking them to a piece of nylon net before subjecting them to the additional strain imposed by the weight of washing water.

3. Has the material been given a mechanical finish that will be destroyed by wetting? Moire and watered silks owe their characteristic patterning to the fact that they have been treated by being passed through heavy rollers, and mercerised cotton and some voiles owe their sheen to the filaments having been polished. Wet a small area before committing the whole article to treatment.

4. What is the nature of the dirt? Is it merely ingrained dust that washing will remove? Is it of an oily or greasy nature? Or stained by iron or other chemical action? There is no point in washing an article when the only thing that will remove the stain is dry-cleaning or special treatment.

Remember the golden rule: when there is any doubt in your mind, *never hesitate to consult an expert*. The conservation staff of your nearest museum will give advice, but always take the article for examination. You do not want to damage beyond restoration a treasured possession, so ask first. As a general rule, remove dust and dirt by vacuum cleaning, but even here caution is required, for too much suction on fragile fabrics can easily cause them to disintegrate. The protection of nylon net is advisable for anything showing signs of weakness.

Where size does not make it impossible, soaking in distilled or softened water is often effective. Clean rainwater is free of hardness which can be harmful to fabrics as it leaves white deposits behind. The article should be laid flat in a bath or large tray containing enough water to cover it and the water should be changed several times until all the dirt has been lifted out. This may take several hours. Avoid any agitation or rubbing with fragile materials and support them on net to facilitate lifting and drying. When clean simply transfer to a flat absorbent bed of sheeting or blotting paper. If water alone will not remove the dirt, it is possible that the addition of spirit soap, which you can obtain from almost any chemist, will assist in the removal of grease and other stains. Use at the strength of 1 oz. to a pint of water, and never rub or scrub the article. Light agitation is all the movement that is safe with fragile materials.

Where washing is unsuitable, cleaning with non-aqueous **solvents** is the next alternative. Nearly all of them are highly flammable and give off vapours that should not be inhaled in high concentration, so use them only in a well-ventilated area well away from any source of ignition. Carbon Tetrachloride is non-flammable but gives off a vapour that becomes a poison if you smoke while using it. It is a good all-round dry cleaning agent. Trichloroethane 🔥 is also excellent and can be used in conjunction with spirit soap ($\frac{1}{2}$ oz. to two pints of the solvent). The addition of spirit soap increases the cleaning power of the dry cleaning agent.

Even with dry cleaning liquids you cannot take if for granted that the colours will not run, painted fabrics particularly can be damaged, so always test first.

FADING – see under item

FANS
There are two types of fan, rigid and folding; it is the folding variety that is most collected and which requires most attention. The oriental rigid fan can be traced back to earliest times, and it was used in both ancient Egypt and Greece. In some parts of the world it has strong religious connotations, although in Europe these disappeared in the Middle Ages. The folding fan is said to have been invented in Japan in the seventh century AD and was

introduced into Europe in the early sixteenth century. In 1673 the guild of Parisian Fan Makers was incorporated, and they were so highly regarded during the seventeenth and eighteenth centuries that famous artists like Watteau and Boucher were commissioned to design them. Queen Victoria was an ardent fan collector and no doubt set the scene for this still popular hobby.

The spokes or struts of fans are made from a variety of materials, such as ivory, tortoiseshell, whalebone, wood and bamboo, and are often ornamented with intricate designs (in 1869 Alphonse Baudet invented machinery for carving them) and are frequently broken. The covering may be of paper, vellum, lace, silk or feathers. Fans are often hand-painted and the colours are not fast, so very great care has to be exercised when attempting cleaning.

First try crumbled breadcrumbs or a very soft India rubber. One of the mild **solvents** such as Carbon Tetrachloride should be carefully tested before general application. Silk and lace fans can often be cleaned satisfactorily with **Fuller's earth**.

The spokes of fans are normally held together at the hub by a rivet or pin. When mending broken spokes, the first task is to remove the rivet. Fortunately they are usually made of soft metals, such as brass, so the enlarged end can fairly easily be filed, or cut off with a pair of wire cutters. Once the spokes are separated, repairs become much easier. If there is a large enough point of contact, broken spokes can be glued together with a rapid drying glue – see **adhesives**. Apply a strip of self-adhesive tape to the back of the break *before* the adhesive to ensure exact alignment and to reinforce the join.

Very slender spokes will need more reinforcement: apply a splint of suitable material to the back. If the spoke is wooden, use a strip of veneer; if it is of ivory or tortoiseshell, rigid plastic. After the repair has set hard, trim the splint down to shape and smooth off the edges. Once reassembled, the repair will be invisible from the front.

If the old rivet is found to be too short, make a new one, using brass or copper wire.

FEATHERS – see STUFFED ANIMALS

FIREARMS

When firearms are in good condition, the only maintenance required is an occasional oiling. Once every six months is sufficient in normal circumstances, but it is important to use the correct grade of rifle oil – see **oils and lubricants**. Remember that locks, springs and other parts of the mechanism not immediately accessible also need occasional attention to prevent rust. A humid atmosphere is sufficient to attack unprotected iron and steel. Sometimes bright steel is lacquered, but this is not recommended, as the finish always looks a bit 'scrummy', or plastic.

When a firearm of any description comes into your possession for the first time, CHECK THAT IT IS NOT LOADED. With muzzle loaders, slide a piece of dowel down the barrel, mark its length and compare it with the outside measurement of the barrel. If it is found to be charged, the greatest care must be taken over removing the ball, wad and powder. If you possess a cleaning rod, it most likely has a screw fitting which can be screwed into the ball. If you like, play safe and take it to a gunsmith.

Newly acquired pieces, unless thoroughly clean, should be stripped down army fashion. First the lock should be removed, usually by unscrewing it from the stock. Screws are likely to be corroded or rusted and great care is needed not to tear the slot where the screwdriver fits. To loosen, see SCREWS. Next to be removed are the barrel, butt cap, ramrod well and trigger guard. These are all secured with either screws or pins. For tapping out pins, use a brass or other soft metal rod. Care is required to ensure that the wooden part of the gun is not splintered.

Once stripped, the first task is the removal of rust. A mixture of paraffin and gun oil is the traditional recipe. Soak the parts at least overnight. Alternatively, if care is required to see that etching of the parts does not take place, use a **rust remover**.

The next process is polishing, and for this you will need several grades of Jeweller's Emery paper. (See **abrasives**.) Start off with a slightly coarse paper and finish with very fine. This will produce a brilliant shine.

All the parts should now be given a thin covering of rifle oil, taking care that you do not handle the parts with bare hands. The fingers will leave a corrosive deposit which will turn into an indelible mark. It is a good idea to wear cheap throw-away surgical gloves, stocked by most chemists.

If the weapon is to be fired, clean the interior of the barrel with a cleaning rod, which will bring it up bright and clean. However, if it is pitted or shows other signs of wear, consult a gunsmith before trying it out.

The wooden parts of the gun will also require cleaning. Fine steel wool (see **abrasives**), lubricated with **solvent** such as white spirit or linseed oil, will remove even heavy grime and dirt. Rub along the grain, not across it, to avoid making superficial scratches. If perished varnish or other persistent grime and dirt is present, use a good **paint stripper** and, following treatment, neutralise with white spirit. Polish butts and stocks with a wax furniture polish.

Dents in wooden parts can often be reduced, or even removed completely, by applying a damp cloth pad or cotton wool to the bruised area. The moisture will cause the fibres of the wood to swell, thus reducing the blemish. This treatment may take two or three days to become effective.

Only a gunsmith can treat the steel parts so as to give them a blue or, less frequently, a brown finish. These processes are highly technical.

Koldblack, made by Jenolite Ltd and distributed by Frank W. Joel Ltd*, chemically produces a layer of black iron oxide on iron and steel and is particularly suitable for arms and armour.

When you have thoroughly cleaned and polished your gun, protect it for reasonably long periods with a **lubricant** – a silicone Rifle oil, or wax polish.

FOXING – see PAPER

FRAMES

Mirror, picture and screen frames can be roughly divided into those having a natural wood or painted finish and those that are gilded. Neglected wall fixtures are the main cause of damage: picture cords and wires perish and sometimes snap. The screw eyes and rings rust in time and often the screw or nail in the wall support proves inadequate. Check these from time to time. Replace cotton or jute cords with nylon, which does not rot. Inspect all such items from time to time.

It may sound obvious, but it is worth stressing that no repairs should be undertaken until picture or mirror glass has been removed.

The most common fault in both kinds of frame, particularly if it has taken a bad knock at some time, is failure of the corner joints. To reglue them, use a P.V.A. **adhesive** or carpenter's glue. (See **adhesives**.) Reinforce the corners where necessary by driving two or more panel pins diagonally through the sides of the frame to hold the two corners together. With larger frames, substitute wooden dowels for the pins. Alternatively screw a metal corner plate, either triangular or right-angled, on to the back of the frame, if you are sure the frame is strong enough to carry it.

When effecting any of these repairs, take great care to ensure that the frame is absolutely square. The best way to achieve this is to use a set square, or an accurate, home-made, right-angled piece. Hardboard is suitable for this.

Wooden or painted frames
Some of the early mirror frames are extremely fragile, and the fretted extremities are liable to snap off with the slightest strain. Very often one or more of these parts will already be missing. Check carefully to make sure that the frame is complete; if not, cut and fit new pieces taken from old wood of the same variety and texture as the rest of the frame. Usually the frame is thick enough for a simple glue joint to hold, but if not, a strip of thick veneer can be stuck to the back as reinforcement. To get the right shape, cut a paper pattern from the identical part on the opposite side of the frame.

Natural wood frames and most painted frames can be cleaned up by a gentle wash in warm water and detergent, once the loose dust and cobwebs have been brushed off. Where possible, apply only one coat of clear **wax polish** to restore the wood to its former condition. Mahogany and maple frames have most likely acquired a patina which must on no account be destroyed by stripping and repolishing.

Always try to preserve the original finish, and only resort to its removal when it has deteriorated beyond resurrection. When this is the case, see Stripping and Repolishing in FURNITURE.

Clean painted frames carefully with a suitable **solvent**: the most appropriate will have to be determined by trial and error, but start with white spirit (which will not dissolve French polish, but will attack some paint if not applied with caution) and then go on to try other **paint strippers** until you find the best. Remember not to over-clean antique frames, otherwise they may finish up looking like reproductions.

Gilt frames
These frames usually have a wooden base, which may or may not be carved. The best are entirely carved but many have their embellishments cast in plaster with wire reinforcing rods to add strength. All gilt frames are coated with gesso – a mixture of glue and whiting – to provide a smooth base and give a key to the layer of gold leaf subsequently applied (see GILDING).

Beneath the gold leaf there is almost invariably a coat of priming colour, usually a rich red, which adds body to the layer of gold. Because of the nature of the preparatory coat, avoid cleaning with an excess of water, and do not use detergents. Careful cleaning with a cotton-wool pad dampened with water containing a little ammonia will remove most surface dirt.

On old gilt frames, some of the gold leaf may have worn away with frequent dusting to reveal traces of the red or crimson undercoat. The effect of this aging is not unpleasant and no attempt should normally be made to 'restore' the gilding. On the other hand, particularly with the cheaper plastered frames, parts may have broken off, revealing unsightly areas of white.

Restore broken mouldings by casting new parts – see **casting**.

Gilding is a highly specialised craft (see GILDING) but a reasonable finish can be obtained by using one of the gilding waxes, obtainable from art shops. They are sold under the names of Goldfinger or Treasure Gold, and come in a variety of shades. You can also buy an excellent product called Treasuregold Liquid Gold

Leaf. All of these products will take a light burnish and can be protected with a clear lacquer.

FRENCH POLISHING – see FURNITURE – FRENCH POLISHING

FURNITURE
Furniture gets just about as much wear and tear as a motor car. Every day it is subjected to stress and exposed to accidental damage: both need polishing, and the outside surfaces need the protection of wax, while working parts call for oiling and greasing. To carry the analogy further, both need protection from the elements, furniture from the dry atmosphere created during the winter months by central heating. Indeed, more damage has been inflicted on antique furniture by central heating than all the wear and tear of the past couple of hundred years. Don't be frightened to tackle repairs to a piece of furniture, just because it is an antique. Again, like motor cars, they need maintenance. Remember, however, that it is very important to preserve the authenticity of good antique furniture. It may be quicker to replace, rather than preserve, a worm-eaten leg on a 200-year-old chair, but replacement will reduce the value by as much as half, while repair will enhance it; if properly done, it will also give it a new lease of serviceable life.

Do not mistake a high polish for patina. Our Victorian forebears were fond of renovating and their ideas do not coincide with ours. Many an eighteenth century piece was sent away to be French Polished with a 'piano finish' after being stained dark purple with one of the new analine dyes.

Before about 1600 most furniture was made from domestic timbers, but oak, having the greatest durability of such woods, it is oak that has survived from Tudor times in the main. More often than not, beeswax was used as a polish base – and there is nothing more beautiful than a pure wax finish, built up over many decades.

From Stuart times until well into the reign of George I walnut was the fashionable wood and linseed oil began to supersede beeswax. By about 1720 Europe had used up most of its walnut wood, but expanding trade led to the introduction of Cuban and Honduras mahogany. This was the golden age of English furniture-making, the century of the Chippendales, Sheraton, Hepplewhite and the Adam brothers. Linseed oil polishing was still common, but towards the end of the eighteenth century resins (such as shellac) were added to the linseed oil, mainly in an attempt to reduce heavy labour costs at the finishing stages.

French polishing was not introduced into Britain until about 1820. It involves the use of successive coats of shellac dissolved in wood alcohol. From around the turn of this century cellulose and other synthetic finishes applied with a spray gun have been mainly used.

FURNITURE CLEANING

Dull and lifeless surfaces can often be revived and brightened up, and this involves cleaning down before waxing. Usually a thorough scrub down with fine steel wool and white spirit will remove both accumulated dirt and old wax without damaging any French polish or varnish surface. Always rub the steel wool (see **abrasives**) in the direction of the grain of the wood and use only the finer grades (000 grade is ideal).

Smeary surfaces can often be cured by less drastic methods, such as wiping over with a soft rag charged with vinegar and warm water, followed by a burnishing with a chamois leather.

A good furniture cleaner can be made up as follows:

Linseed oil	
Vinegar	4 parts of each
Real turpentine	
Methylated spirit	1 part

This mixture can be rubbed over the surface, but use it sparingly until you have developed a familiarity with its use. Methylated spirit melts French polish, so an excess of the cleaner left on a polished surface for too long will do more harm than good.

Bone keyholes – see BONE

Boulle – see BOULLE

Brass fittings – see BRASS AND COPPER FITTINGS

Handles – see BRASS AND COPPER FITTINGS

Inkstains – see below under *Persistent stains*

Persistent stains
To remove these usually involves the complete removal of surface polishing. Some of the original stains as well as some of the accidental blemishes, such as ink marks, can be removed by **paint strippers**, but persistent stains will require special attention. The easiest-to-use **stain remover** is Oxalic acid. This white, crystalline substance is obtainable from chemists. Dissolve 2 heaped tablespoons in a quart of warm water. It is most effective if applied hot, but you can keep the solution in a labelled jar for later use; it is quite effective when cold. Pour some of the liquid on to the ink mark or other type of stain and, before it has a chance to run over the edge, start to scrub it into the surface with a pad of wire wool. Scrub only in direction of the grain to avoid visible scratching. In order to avoid having a lighter area where the stain once was, an application of Oxalic acid will have to be made over the complete surface, but obviously most of the rubbing will be concentrated in the area of stains. Once you are convinced that as much of the stain has been removed as is going to come out, stop rubbing and allow the surface to remain wet for a few minutes, but do not allow it to dry out completely as the surface residue is unpleasant and makes you sneeze. Just before the area has dried out, wash it over well with plenty of clean water and then allow it to dry. This will take at least 24 hours in spite of the fact that it will appear to be dry in an hour or so. In nearly all cases the stains will have disappeared or been reduced to such an extent that an application of new stain will render them almost invisible.

Rings and stains
The most common cause of rings on the surface of polished
furniture is either (a) heat marks; (b) alcohol marks or (c) water
marks. Unfortunately there is no magic wand that can be used to
eradicate these unsightly blemishes and success in their removal will
depend on the degree of penetration into the polished surface.
All successful treatment depends on a combination of frictional heat
with mild abrasives and lubricants. Grandmother's remedies are
often effective, such as cigarette or cigar ash mixed with saliva
rubbed into the area of the blemish with a finger covered with a
clean cotton rag. Alternatively camphorated oil, linseed oil, or olive
oil mixed with any mild abrasive, such as fine Pumice powder, will
have the same effect. Brass or silver polishes can also be used, but
with caution as they contain a percentage of wood alcohol which is a
solvent for French polish and may destroy the surface.
Commercially formulated remedies, such as Topp's Ringaway may
also be tried and will be effective if the damage is not too great.

  Where major penetration of the skin of polish has occurred, the
best solution is to strip the entire surface and repolish. This is often
quicker and easier than trying to polish in a small area only.

Upholstery – see FABRICS

Veneer – see FURNITURE REPAIRS *Veneers*

FURNITURE – FRENCH POLISHING
French polishing was introduced into England in about 1820, when
it superseded varnish polishing. Today, the Victorian fashion of
producing a 'piano finish' on furniture by applying dozens of coats
of shellac is no longer favoured. The current trend is to apply only a
few coats of French polish to antique furniture, leaving the grain
visible and providing no more than a 'shellac seal' as a basis for wax
polishing.

  Today the availability of new and very cleverly formulated
materials allows you to achieve professional results. The method is
closely allied to traditional French polishing, but a harder, more
durable, surface is produced. Use Furniglas Home French Polish,

French polishing

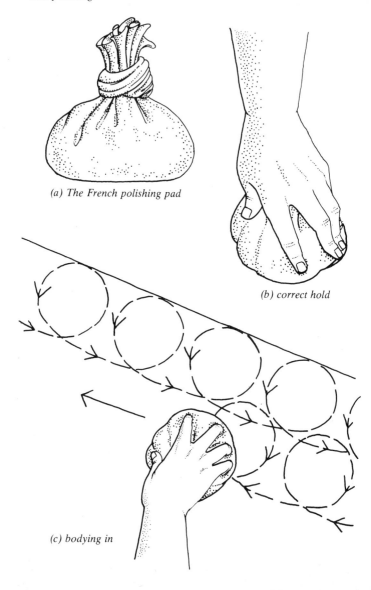

(a) The French polishing pad

(b) correct hold

(c) bodying in

widely available in DIY packs. These contain two liquids: a specially formulated French polish (Furniglas No. 1) and a finishing, buffing and hardening medium (Furniglas No. 2). The only occasion when it is not suitable is on very light woods, when Furniglas Colourless Polish should be substituted. Full instructions for the application of Furniglas are of course enclosed with each pack but, in addition, you will require the following: a few sheets of sandpaper (9/0 Garnet or Lubrasil non-clog paper); a piece of cotton wool about 7–10 ins square; soft, fluff-free cotton rag (old sheets are ideal); methylated spirit; and a cork sanding-block to hold the sandpaper.

There are four stages in the application of French polishing. You must:

(1) build up an even coating of polish on the surface by repeated and fairly generous applications of polish;
(2) when dry, sand down lightly;
(3) apply the second and final coating of Furniglas No. 1 with long strokes, using a relatively dry pad;
(4) burnish and harden the surface with Furniglas No. 2.

Before applying any French polish, examine the piece of furniture very carefully. Make sure it is now entirely free from dust, dirt and any remnant of old polish. Remember, perfection depends on a perfect foundation, so a final check for overlooked blemishes will save regrets later.

Ensure that the room in which you are working is warm (at least above 60°F/16°C) and is dust free. In cold temperatures, French polish tends to bloom and turn milky. Dust is the great enemy of the French polisher.

Protect your hands with a barrier cream or wear a pair of disposable surgical gloves. Thick rubber gloves are not as good, as they reduce the feeling that you need at your fingertips.

Now make a polishing pad out of cotton wool about 7–10 ins square, folding it first into a triangle and then turning the corners in to produce a ball. Place this pad in a square of clean cotton rag, giving the ends and sides a twist, which is held in the palm out of the way. Extend your fingers and grasp the pad with your fingertips. Practise this before wetting the pad with polish. The cotton wool acts as a reservoir for the French polish, while the rag holds the pad together and keeps fluff from the surface when polishing. By increasing or decreasing the pressure of your fingers, you regulate the flow of the polish. Now unfold the rag and moisten the cotton wool with methylated spirit . Place the opened triangle of cotton wool on the rag in the centre of your outstretched palm. Wet the cotton wool liberally with French polish, fold in the corners and fold up into a ball as described previously.

You are now ready to use Furniglas No. 1. Apply the liquid methodically in a series of tight circular movements, each one overlapping the last. As the polish dries almost instantly, apply successive coats immediately. Take care, however, to ensure that no blobs or dribbles are left behind. Go back immediately to mop up any surplus polish left on the surface.

On most woods used for furniture, three or four coats are sufficient for surface sealing, but apply as many coats as you wish until the required depth of polish is achieved. After a maximum of about a dozen coats, let the work stand for a while to harden. Now sand over lightly with Garnet or Lubrasil paper.

Having built up the depth of polish required, you come to stage (3). With a drier and firmer pad – one which will leave no wet patches or ridges of polish – apply the second coat with long, graceful strokes of even weight. Vary the place where the pad comes into contact with the surface on every stroke, and continue the sweep beyond the end of the polished area. Wherever possible polish in the same direction as the grain.

Once you are satisfied, set the work aside for at least three hours, during which time the surface will consolidate and harden.

It is now time for stage (4). You will see that the surface is shiny and brash: this is because there is too much reflection of light. Furniglas No. 2 gives the work a mellowness and depth while imparting added hardness. Wet a pad of cotton wool generously with it, after thoroughly shaking up the container. Polish one manageable strip at a time and, exerting pressure, rub with the grain about 20 times over. Next, while the section is still moist, polish with a clean duster until the surface is dry; this completes the process. Remember, regular wax polishing will enhance and improve the polish over the years and protect and feed the wood. Remember, too, that excessive exposure to sunlight or to a fire or radiator will accelerate deterioration of the finish.

French polish revivers
Some French polished surfaces become perished, either by excessive exposure to sunlight or heat, or by natural deterioration of imperfect polishing. A common condition is crazing, where the surface polish shows hundreds of tiny cracks.

Normally it is quicker and easier to strip off the whole surface and repolish, but if for some reason this course is impractical, reviving the surface finish can be attempted.

A number of specially formulated products are available, such as Topp's Ringaway, Rustin's Polish Reviver, Gedge's Durax Reviver (obtainable direct from them) and Furniglas No. 2 (in the French Polish pack). Alternatively you can make up your own reviving solution:

Real turpentine	2 parts
Linseed oil	2 parts
Methylated spirit	5 parts.

Work over the surface with a pad of soft cotton material, using a circular motion. This softens the surface and allows it to flow slightly, thus filling up the cracks and reducing the crazing.

Revivers are sometimes effective for the removal of rings and stains caused by spilt drinks, flower vases, hot plates, etc. You will, however, find that they will only work if the damage is relatively superficial. If the alcohol or watermark has penetrated the polished surface, see FURNITURE CLEANING – RINGS AND STAINS.

FURNITURE POLISHING
The ideal finish for any piece of natural wood furniture is a deep glowing wax polish. In order to achieve this the best method is to use a solid wax polish containing a high proportion of beeswax.

While it is easy to make up your own wax polish (a recipe is given below) it may be prudent to consider that the time required to achieve the requisite shine will outweigh the money saved on proprietary polishes.

There is a wide choice of polishes on the market that their manufacturers have spent years of research in perfecting. They contain a blend of hard waxes and quick drying solvents which produce a quick durable shine. Select one of the solid brands that the maker recommends for use on antique furniture. You will find that they are produced in a range of colours from natural to dark brown, so if you want to tone a piece of furniture the coloured waxes should be selected.

Furniture creams and oils are designed for removing surface dust and cleaning furniture, or for use on modern furniture which has a sprayed synthetic surface, so do not use it on antiques, except for removing excessive polish, dust and grime. Aerosols are a waste of money, even if they are easy to use. The bulk of the contents is propellant gas that polishes nothing.

Wax polish should be liberally applied three or four times a year. The rest of the time burnishing with a soft cloth is all that needs doing. An old short-haired paintbrush or a shoe brush is a useful applicator for carved furniture. Cover the entire surface before going back to start polishing with a soft cloth. As the shine begins to appear, change over to a clean cloth and rub only in the direction of the grain.

If you encounter scratches, these can often be concealed and polished away by applying the right shade of boot polish. This is a tip widely used in the antique and modern furniture trades and is very effective. Another useful hint is to polish over brass handles and other fittings with wax polish. This will seal the surface so that oxidization is retarded and the brass stays bright.

Homemade wax polish
Shred about a pound of beeswax on a vegetable shredder and pack lightly into a double boiler. Add sufficient real turpentine to just cover the lightly packed flakes of wax and enough carbon black to cover a penny piece.

Heat carefully as the solvent is flammable, and when liquid stir to distribute the constituents evenly. Pour into a suitable container to cool and harden. It should be soft enough for you to be able to stick your finger into the finished polish, leaving a permanent indentation.

FURNITURE REPAIRS

The following instructions call for the minimum of tools and materials and can be carried out without a workshop. Leave major repairs to a competent restorer. If you can't find one contact your County Advisory Officer at CoSIRA* who hold lists of craftsmen, among them your nearest furniture restorer.

Tools
Essential tools in the following list have been italicised.

Bench	Bench Hook
	Vice
	Mitre box
Saws	Rip Saw (cutting with grain) 4 points to inch
	Panel Saw (cutting across wood) 10 points to inch
	Tenon Saw (cutting joints) 14–16 points to inch
	Gents Saw (small cuts) 20–32 points to inch
	Coping Saw (cutting curves and holes)
	Padsaw
	Fretsaw
Hammers	*Claw hammer 16–20 oz*
	Cross Pein hammer 8–10 oz
	Tack hammer or Pin hammer
	Pin Push
	Set of punches
Planes	Joiners Plane
	Jack Plane
	Smooth Plane
	Block Plane

	Shoulder Plane
	Combination Plane
Chisels	*Bevel Edge Chisels* $\frac{1}{4}''$ $\frac{1}{2}''$ $\frac{3}{4}''$ $1''$
	Firmer Gouge $\frac{1}{2}''$
	Mortice Chisel $\frac{1}{2}''$
	Oilstone (India) fine or medium
	Honing Guide
	Spokeshave
	Stanley Knife
Rasps	*Sandpaper Block*
	Flat Surform
	Small Surform
	10″ Halfround rasp
	Cylindrical rasp
	Cabinet Scraper
	Two rifflers
Screwdrivers	Heavy Screwdriver 20″
	Medium Screwdriver (London pattern) 14″
	Small Screwdriver 6″
	Midget Screwdriver 3″
	Awl
Bradawl	
	Wheel Brace
	Set twist drills
	Countersink bit
Try Square	
	Marking Gauge
	Mortice Gauge
Straight Edge	
Rule 2 ft	
10 ft tape	
6 G Cramps	
	Pliers
2 Sash Cramps	
	Pincers
2 Chisel Scrapers 1″ and 2″	

Power Tools   Two speed drill
                     Bandsaw
                     Lathe attachment
                     Circular saw attachment and table
                     Grindstone
                     Face grinder

Beading – see BEADING AND STRINGING

Boulle – see BOULLE

Bruises and dents

Soak out with water for 24 to 36 hours. Use wet tissue or muslin.

Castors
Where the wood has been cut away or has rotted away to such an extent that original fittings, such as castors, can no longer be held on securely, pack the enlarged cavity with a **filler** such as Plastic Padding or Isopon. Replace the castor and, when dry, the part becomes cemented in. As these fillers are coloured, you may need a coat of paint for an exact match.

Chair legs
When chair legs are of uneven length, rather than trying to even them up by cutting the other ones down, build up the short one by gluing or screwing on a slip of hardwood. Cutting down very often results in finishing up with a chair of nursing height which once was for dining!

Where the break is clean and new, such breaks can often be repaired by simply gluing together with a strong **adhesive** such as Cascamite. If the repair seems insecure, it can sometimes be reinforced with a wooden dowel. When a leg is very weak, first make a repair by gluing the elements together; when the glue is dry, saw the leg in half just above or below the repair and reinforce the leg by drilling out both sections to accommodate a long dowel in the centre of the leg to bear the stresses of everyday use.

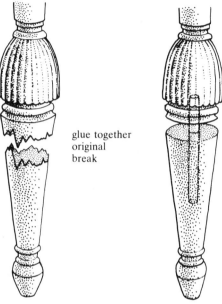

glue together
original
break

saw through
in new
place and
insert
dowel

Repairing a broken table leg

Cock beads – see BEADING AND STRINGING

Damage through damp to legs and feet
This job is too complicated for the amateur, and should be left to
the professional restorer.

Drawer runners
Have you ever looked at a chest-of-drawers and felt that, in spite of
it being in good superficial repair and well polished, there is
something wrong with it? Next time take a second look and observe
whether the drawers all tip backwards slightly. If they do, this is due
to the drawer runners having worn. Drawer runners always wear

out much more quickly at the back than the front; this causes the drawer to tilt backwards, a sure sign that it is high time the runners were replaced.

All but the earliest drawers dating back to the first part of the seventeenth century are constructed so that they run on two strips of wood which are extensions of the sides. Depending on the weight of things inside and the frequency of their opening and closing, these runners wear out and at the same time cut channels in the drawer dividers.

The rate of wear and tear can be reduced considerably if the runners are lubricated about once a year by rubbing them with the butt of a candle. The coating of wax reduces the friction and makes the drawers run much more easily.

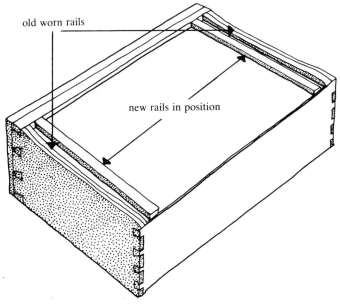

old worn rails

new rails in position

Replacing old drawer runners

In many cases there is a very easy solution for correcting the fault: where the drawer dividers are wide enough, glue a new runner to the bottom of the drawer, tight against the old worn runner. (Any type of wood glue such as a P.V.A., Evostik Resin 'W', will do.) The new runner thus does not run in the worn groove of the drawer rail and in consequence the drawer no longer tilts back or binds when opened or shut. Do not nail these new runners into place, as in time they too will wear, but the nail head will not, and there is nothing so disastrous as a proud nail-head to wreck a drawer divider.

Drawer stops
Some drawers are prevented from sliding too far into the body of a piece of furniture by small blocks of wood fixed to the drawer dividers. These stops, which take quite a beating, often get knocked off or so badly worn that the drawer over-rides them. The positioning of new stops is critical, and measuring – rather than guesswork – will prevent frustration. Use a mortice gauge if you have one.

The thickness of the piece of wood forming the front of the drawer can easily be measured, and this measurement transferred to the place where the new drawer stop has to be fixed. Mark the place for the front edge of the stop with a pencil and then glue (with any wood glue) and pin it into position. Make sure all the excess glue is wiped away before replacing the drawer, or you may find that it is permanently closed!

Feet
The feet of various types of furniture are quite often found to have sustained water damage from frequent floor washing or rising damp. In extreme cases rotting or spongy, insecure feet result.

If at all possible, avoid replacing. Often regluing and pinning are all that is required. Of course the feet must be thoroughly dried out. Rickety feet can be reinforced by gluing an additional wooden support (with any wood glue) at the back of bracket or similar feet. If the original weight-bearing foot is missing (a frequent occurrence), it should be replaced by a new one a fraction longer than the rest of the feet, so that it will carry the weight.

Some chair-legs, or similar slender legs and feet, can be
reinforced by carefully drilling out the centre of the leg to a depth of
several inches and inserting as large a dowel as practical, again a
fraction longer than the original leg.

When legs are uneven, do not try to make the article stand firm
by sawing bits off the longer legs. Level it *up* by gluing a piece of
wood of suitable size and thickness on to the shorter leg. This will
save considerable frustration.

Handles
It is almost impossible to find old original brass fittings, and if
handles are missing or badly broken, reproduction handles will have
to be used. These can be obtained through suppliers such as
Beardmores.* (Look also in your local Yellow Pages.)

Hinges
These can work loose, usually because the holes of the screws that
hold them in place have become enlarged: in extreme cases the
wood may by split to such an extent that there is no hope of getting
new screws to hold. In the case of enlarged screw holes, first remove
the hinge and then plug the enlarged holes with tapered plugs made
from deal or similar softwood. It is best to glue these plugs in place.
(Use any wood glue.) The ends are cut off flush with the surface
with a sharp chisel. Make a new hole to start the screw with a
bradawl and replace the hinge with the *correct* size of screw. The
head of the screw should fit flush into the countersunk screwhole.
Too large a screw will stand proud and stress both the hinge and the
wood to which it is secured; too small and it will work loose in no
time.

When the wood is split, sometimes it can be glued back into place,
using any wood glue. If it is too far gone, a new piece will have to be
inlaid which is solid enough to stand the stress exerted by the screws
and hinge.

Locks – see LOCKS

Moulding – see BEADING

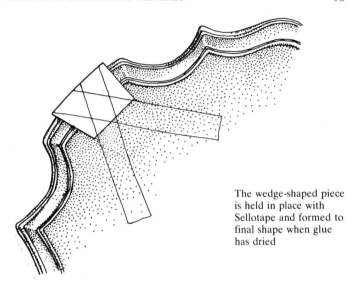

The wedge-shaped piece is held in place with Sellotape and formed to final shape when glue has dried

Repairing a pie crust table

Shrinkage and cracking

To fill cracks, splits, etc., when renovating furniture, use Brummer stopper – a filler formulated in various colours. It is smooth, thins in water and does not shrink on drying.

Shrinkage and cracking often occur with old furniture even though it has been well looked after and in consequence has acquired a beautiful patina that it would be a crime to disturb. On these occasions, fill the gaps with a hard wax filler which will neither disturb the surface nor in any way damage the valuable piece of furniture.

Splits, breaks and holes

Some furniture, particularly that built from solid wood, develops splits or cracks when it gets old. Repairing depends on the size and nature of the fault. It is, as always, essential to clean all dirt and grease out of any crack before attempting any repair. Small cracks can often be pulled together with a sash cramp after glue has been spread inside the split. In the case of large cracks, the best course is to insert a sliver of wood suitably tapered to the shape of the split and glue and cramp it in place. After the glue has dried, the cramps can be removed and the excess wood planed off and smoothed until the surface is level.

Provided they are in unobtrusive places, fill small splits and holes with one of the patent stoppers such as Brummer: they come in various shades, but they can also be coloured and concealed with stains or pigments. Holes in table tops and other flat surfaces where the light strikes across them cannot be filled satisfactorily, as the repair shows up invariably. Consult an expert.

Veneers
Veneers are thin sheets of wood, usually expensive, and beautifully figured, which are stuck with glue to the outer surfaces of a piece of furniture made from less expensive wood. Little if any veneering was done in this country before the Restoration (1660) and the reason for its popularity was the interesting patterns that were produced when the logs of wood were sawn across to produce burr walnut, for instance, or when smaller limbs were sawn at an oblique angle to produce oyster configuration as with laburnum and again walnut.

In both England and Europe walnut supplies became exhausted to such an extent that an embargo was placed on exports from France in 1720 and supplies from other sources, such as Virginia and Spain were insufficient to satisfy the demand. This shortage undoubtedly contributed to the widespread use of veneers for the production of walnut furniture, and increased the use of veneers cut from branches, even small ones; every little part of a walnut tree had to be used to conserve the precious and expensive timber.

Before the advent of power-driven machinery veneers were cut by hand sawing, as many as 8 sheets being obtained from an inch thickness of timber. Today, and since Victorian times, veneers have been cut with a knife and are much thinner than the earlier hand-cut examples which often vary in thickness in the same sheet.

It was the shortage of supplies of walnut which made the British cabinet-makers of the first quarter of the eighteenth century turn to mahogany as an alternative. In the year 1753 more than 5,000,000 cubic feet of mahogany were sent to this country through Jamaica.

Since the thickness of antique veneers can vary considerably from those of today, it is important to preserve broken pieces and glue them back in place as soon as possible if a lot of extra work is to be avoided. Resist the temptation to put the bit of veneer away in a safe place to be glued back later: it is too easy to forget the safe place and delay the repair until the piece is lost. Rather, secure it temporarily in place with a strip of Sellotape until the permanent repair can be made.

Should a piece of veneer be missing, you are faced with the problem of where to find suitable replacements. Most professional restorers cut their own veneers to obtain a good match of both grain and colour; if you have a restorer in the district, this is the first place to try. Many shops sell marquetry sets and small pieces of veneers of many woods, and this is another possible source of supply. Or look in the Classified Trades Directory under Veneer Merchants.

You may have to use thinner veneers for your repairs than those originally used. In this case you laminate two or even three layers together. But always try to use a veneer thicker than the original one; then after the glue has set the new piece can be planed and sanded down to the exact height.

When repairing broken and jagged areas, cut away the uneven edges with a sharp, thin, bladed knife. A Stanley knife is ideal. When making clean edges for the repair, follow the pattern of the grain wherever possible. When you have to cut across the grain, make the cut an easy curve, rather than a straight line. This will render the finished repair less detectable as the eye picks up a straight line much more easily than a curve.

Next carefully clean away all the old glue and dirt that may still be adhering to the repair area. This can usually be done by scraping with a chisel blade, though you may have to wash persistent glue away. Now, make a paper pattern of the required shape: This is done by placing a piece of paper over the area and lightly scribbling

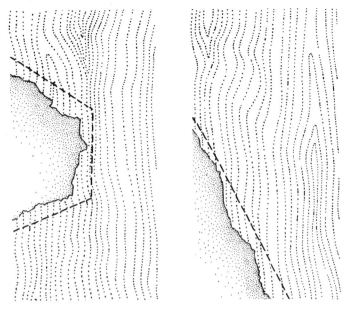

(a) Cut out a suitably shaped area with smooth sides

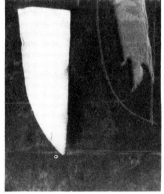

(b) Make paper template to fit space

(c) Cut out new piece of veneer with Stanley knife and fit

over the surface with a lead pencil, thus producing an outline of the
cavity. The pattern is now cut out with a pair of scissors and fitted
into the cavity to ensure a perfect fit. Glue the pattern on to a
suitable piece of veneer and cut out the shape with a sharp knife,
undercutting the joining edges very slightly, so leaving a small
surplus on the overhanging edge. Finally fit the new piece, adjusting
it where necessary with fine sandpaper held flat on a block of cork
or wood. When you are sure of the fit, glue into place. The paper
pattern need not be removed until the glue has hardened. In most
cases a P.V.A. **adhesive**, such as Borden or Evo-Stick Resin 'W' is
best, but for small repairs use an Acrylic such as UHU. Hold the
repair firmly in place with Sellotape or, if it is a big repair, clamp it
until the glue is thoroughly dry.

Veneers: bubbles and blisters
When veneered furniture is subjected to extremes of temperature
or moisture, movement takes place between the carcass wood and
the veneer, sometimes causing it to break free from the securing
glue. By tapping your finger nails on suspect surfaces you can detect
where veneers have broken free by the hollow sound.

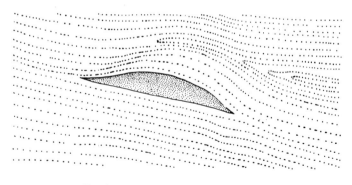

slice through, work in glue if necessary,
and iron down

Treating a veneer bubble

Old and perished glue can often be revived and the loose areas
stuck back again by applying a combination of heat and moisture
with an iron and a damp cloth, much in the same way as creases
used to be put back into flannel trousers. This treatment is likely to
destroy the surface polish which will have to be replaced.

Sometimes bubbles are so badly distorted, or the veneer has
swollen so much that it will not shrink back to its original shape. In
this case make a cut, following the grain of the wood, for the full
length of the blister. This will allow one edge of the veneer to
override the other when ironing down. Where the glue is so far gone
that it cannot be revitalised a similar cut is necessary. Introduce new
adhesive on a palette knife or on a slip of scrap veneer beneath the
lifted veneer. A warm iron will hasten the drying time to less than a
minute if fast-drying Acrylic **adhesive** is used.

On occasion, sections of ornamental stringing or cross-bandings
are missing. Although these can be purchased from veneer
merchants, almost invariably an exact match for anything other than
plain borders cannot be obtained. It is easiest therefore to inlay a
piece of sycamore or similar light-coloured wood of suitable grain
and paint or draw the pattern in with ballpoint or felt-tip pens of
suitable colour. When polished over it is amazing how invisible such
repairs become.

Paint strippers can be used with confidence on veneered furniture
without danger of lifting the veneers, but take care in cases where
veneers are already loose. These will have to be stuck back in place
eventually, and the pieces must not be broken or lost.

Warping
One of the most difficult problems frequently encountered is that of
warped wood in tables, bureaux fronts and the like. This happens
because the moisture content of the wood changes, owing to the
conditions in which the piece of furniture is kept – central heating is
the greatest cause. Attempts at repair through steaming and wetting
will produce only temporary results, and it is best for the amateur to
leave well alone.

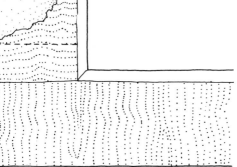

Cross-banding repair

(a) Cut away broken section with neat straight lines

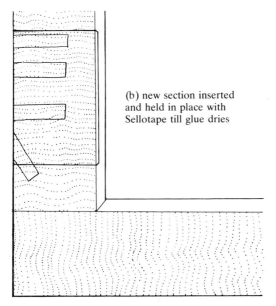

(b) new section inserted and held in place with Sellotape till glue dries

Webbing

This basic support for upholstered seats comes in two qualities: plain hessian, which is cheaper and less durable and black and white patterned cotton which is the more durable.

In time it naturally starts to sag and finally disintegrate. Unfortunately to tighten it up all the upholstery has to be removed and new webbing has to be stretched and tacked securely to the chair rails.

There is really no satisfactory short cut, although some sagging seats can be temporarily repaired by nailing a suitable shaped piece of plywood or hardboard on to the underside of the chair rails.

Woven webbing for the underside of a seat

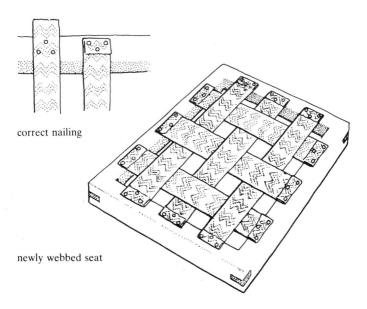

correct nailing

newly webbed seat

Woodworm damage

Active woodworm can be detected by the appearance of little piles of sawdust in the springtime. Since the introduction of modern woodworm insecticides treatment is a simple and permanent matter. Any of the proprietary woodworm solutions will give permanent protection, although you must expect a further emergence of adult beetles the following spring.

The emergence holes of woodworms, long departed, can be filled with either coloured wax polish (boot polish will do very well) or one of the patent fillers, such as Brummer Stopper. It is fairly rare for woodworm to be active in antique furniture, although it is sometimes reintroduced when repairs, such as new backs to chests of drawers, are effected with infested three-ply.

Mahogany, teak and oak heartwood are not attacked by woodworm, but other timbers, particularly walnut and pine, often are.

FURNITURE – STAINING AND COLOURING

Today a light honey or hay colour is considered to be the most acceptable colouring for mahogany furniture, a warm brown for oak and a contrasting brown-to-honey for walnut.

Finishes should look as natural as possible, and any antique or near antique piece of furniture should have the warm sheen of persistent waxing and constant care. There are, of course exceptions to this crude rule of thumb Cuban Mahogany will never fade to a hay colour for instance, but on occasion some bleaching-out of colour may be called for. A variety of bleaches are available, but as an all-purpose standby, oxalic acid is recommended. Alternatives are Peroxide of Hydrogen, household bleaches and when extreme measures are called for, specially formulated professional wood bleaching chemicals, obtainable from one of the wood finishing suppliers.

Two main types of wood colouring stains are available, one based on water solutions and the other on spirit or naphtha. Waterbased stains are those traditionally used in the past and they have a chemical as well as a dyeing action which makes the colour fast. However they also have the disadvantage of tending to lift the grain of the wood and taking longer to dry out to their final colour.

This disadvantage is not found with spirit stains and modern wood colouring dyes are not particularly subject to fading. They can therefore be used with confidence. There are several ranges of proprietary wood stains on the market, based mainly on aniline dyes. They are sold under the names of different woods, and this is misleading as, for instance, a Light Oak stain is not designed to stain only oak, but to impart a light brown colour to any variety of wood. See **wood stains**.

To colour furniture successfully you need a range of colours which can be blended together to obtain the desired effect. Be careful when you buy ready-mixed stains that they do not contain any varnish or other sealing agent. These are usually sold as varnish stains and you want flat colours.

The process of staining is one of the most subtle operations of furniture renovation. It is an art that only experience and practice makes perfect. As a general rule, the less stain that is used on antique furniture the better. In many cases the best result is achieved by using no stain at all and relying on the contrasting shade differences to emphasise the very antiquity of the piece of furniture.

Start off with a very light colour, say yellow oak and build up to the desired shade with successive applications of increasingly darker stains containing those hues which you wish to appear in the finished wood. At the same time you can put in the desired shading at the corners of drawers and in recesses in mouldings and carving to achieve the very desirable variation of colour which goes with antique furniture.

Apply stains with a cotton wool pad. This avoids leaving tell-tale brush marks and ensures an even distribution of the stain.

Certain woods used for inlays and stringing, such as boxwood, holly and tulipwood are almost completely impervious to stains at normal dilutions, so where inlaid furniture has to be re-coloured, you need not fear spoiling the pattern by applying stains. Where these colour-resistant woods have to be toned to match after repairs or replacements, they can be coloured with *either* concentrated solutions of stain in meths or by using pigmented paints.

FURNITURE – STRIPPING PAINT AND VARNISH

The commonest mistake made by amateurs is to apply the **paint stripper** as if it were paint, and brush it out to produce a smooth surface. This only reduces the efficiency of the stripper, resulting in the need to apply more coats before the article is clean. Get as much of it on to the article as will stick and leave it until the varnish, polish or paint has started to swell and cockle up.

Remove the first layer or so with a chisel scraper, taking care not to damage the surface of the wood. You will have to make several applications to remove every vestage of the old finish as it is important that the article is absolutely clear of paint or varnish before starting to repolish.

When removing the last coat or two of the applied stripper, replace the scraper with a ball of the coarsest steel wool (see **abrasives**). Surprisingly this treatment will not completely remove all the patination. Only use it in the direction of the grain; if you scrub across the grain you will scratch the surface. Clean out the carved and awkward corners with a combination of wire wool and sharpened pieces of scrap wood.

After stripping has been completed, wipe over the surfaces thoroughly with white spirit to neutralise the residue of the stripper. Now, while the surface is wet, you can see the colour the wood will be when repolished.

Milk paint

Modern strippers will remove very nearly everything with the exception of milk paint. This was a home-made product, popular in country districts during the eighteenth century and earlier, and was made by mixing boiled-down buttermilk and animal blood. The casein content renders it impervious to most paint strippers and it only responds to a strong ammonia solution. Scrub in with wire wool and leave to soak. The resulting treacly mass can be washed and then scraped off, using wire wool to remove the last vestiges. Sometimes milk paint was made without the addition of blood, and is found as a cream or grey coat on cottage furniture. This finish looks quite effective. To brighten it up mix powdered skimmed milk with water until it is the consistency of emulsion paint, and apply two coats.

GERMAN SILVER – see NICKEL SILVER

GESSO
Gesso is the traditional paste made of whiting or chalk and glue
used by craftsmen throughout the years for a variety of purposes for
filling holes and smoothing surfaces as a base for decoration to
building up relief decoration on such articles as mirror frames.
Gesso is used diluted with water to a thin gruel consistency as a filler
of grain: thicker as a base for painting and gilding: as a paste for
filling in missing detail and modelling and as a stiffish dough for
modelling in such features as floral decoration on frames. Today
modern alternatives based on plastics are more convenient to use
and require less time in preparation.

However, if you wish to make your own, first grind ordinary
whiting to a fine paste with water to remove any trace of lumpy
particles. The paste should be the same consistency as thick cream
and to this should be added enough scotch glue to reduce it to the
texture of a thin pouring cream. Lastly, add a few drops of raw
linseed oil (about 3 drops per egg cupful) and mix well.

Broken or missing areas can then be built up again with
successive coats of the Gesso to their original height and allowed to
dry thoroughly before rubbing down with fine garnet paper to a
marble smooth, polished finish. Where original gesso has become
detached from the base woodwork due to shrinkage, new gesso can
be worked in underneath with a palette knife and cracks can be
filled in similarly.

Where large areas are to be restored, the gesso should be scraped
down with a square edged steel scraper. At all times the surfaces
must be dust free and should be wiped down with a damp cloth. This
applies equally to partly completed work as well as to old damaged
surfaces.

Once the gesso has been restored and rubbed down, the surface
has to be sized with a white pigment base, ground with real
turpentine and finally mixed into goldsize. In all cases, grinding can
either be done in a small mortar with a pestle, or on a white ceramic
tile with a palette knife. The best white pigment to use is Titanium,
because it gives better cover. A few spots of blue can be added, to
indicate that you have achieved complete cover with your sizeing

coat. When this coat is dry, rub down with wire wool.

GILDING

Mirrors, picture frames and furniture have all enjoyed from time to time the fashion of being covered with gold. Traditionally this is achieved by sticking extremely thin sheets of gold leaf to a surface prepared with GESSO, using either paste or gold size as an adhesive. Sometimes only part of the surface is gilded and this is called parcel gilding (partial gilding).

If it is suffering from prolonged neglect, clean the gilding by wiping over with a duster dampened with household ammonia. Take great care with persistent stains, as it is easy to lift and destroy the layer of gold leaf and the prepared base will be damaged by over-exposure to water.

Renovating the areas where the gilding has either been rubbed off or chipped is our first concern. The best repair is to apply new gold leaf to the damaged areas, a highly skilled operation. Fortunately there are simple remedies available that do not call for great craftmanship. The rubbed areas where the gold has gone reveal a red – or sometimes yellow – undercoat, the purpose of which was to give depth and body to the gold leaf. First, stand back and consider whether the 'antique' look of the article is not part of its charm; decide how much renovation is required. Where parts are chipped off, consider if it is advisable to fill them in before applying a coat of gold, remembering that, if you don't, the chip will still show through.

If you decide to fill the chips in, use one of the modern, ready-made **fillers** like Polyfilla, Tetrion or Unifilla. Slightly overfill and, when dry, rub down with fine sandpaper.

The easiest materials to use for minor repairs are gilding waxes, obtainable from most art shops. They come in various shades and it is important to get the nearest match. Rowney's product is called Goldfinger, Reeves' Restoration Wax and Winsor & Newton sell Treasure Wax. Before applying the gilding wax, if there was originally an underlying colour, match it with a similar coat of water-colour or poster paint. Apply the gilding wax either with a finger or with a piece of rag. Buff with a soft brush to give a reasonable lustre and, if required, this can then be rubbed away to show some of the coloured undercoat to give the impression of age. This is called 'distressing'.

Winsor & Newton also sell Treasure Liquid Leaf, which is the only satisfactory gold paint which, after application, does not look like gold paint with its characteristic dull, lifeless texture. Other alternatives are gold aerosols, produced to paint shoes. When using these, take care to mask off areas which must not be painted, bearing in mind that with an aerosol you can shade one hue into another where the match is not exact.

After applying any of these finishes, protect them with a coat of clear varnish, obtainable from art shops.

The intrepid and deft may care to attempt oil gilding. It takes much more time and produces a more satisfactory result. The technique is as follows:

First repair all the surfaces and rub them down so that they are perfectly smooth. Apply the correct colour undercoat, and when that also is thoroughly dry apply a coat of either four-hour goldsize or Japan goldsize. This coat has to be left until the surface is almost dry but still tacky. The art is to catch the goldsize at just the right time. If it is too dry the gold leaf will not adhere, if too wet the leaf will cockle up and wrinkle.

The easiest gold leaf to use is Transfer gold, each sheet of which is lightly held by wax on a piece of tissue paper which makes handling much easier. Gold leaf comes in books of 25 sheets measuring about 2 × 3 inches. The leaf is applied so that each leaf slightly overlaps the preceding one, each join being in the same direction. Light pressure from a cotton pad will transfer the leaf from the tissue to the work.

Gild mouldings and carving in the same way. Using an artist's oil brush of suitable size, press the gold into the corners and then, rubbing in the direction of the overlap, blend fragments from the sheet together to produce an evenly covered surface.

Single sheet oil gilding cannot be burnished, but quite a good match to burnished work can be produced by double thickness gilding. To do this apply a thin coat of wax polish to the newly gilded surface as soon as it has been laid and polish it lightly with a soft shoe brush. As soon as the wax is barely dry apply a second coat of gold leaf. The second coat adheres to the tacky wax. Burnish with a stiff bristle brush or, if you have one, an agate burnisher.

Gold leaf borders on leather desk tops, book bindings, etc., are applied by transferring from a gold strip with a heated brass patterned wheel engraved with a continuous design.

Gold leaf illumination and gold figures are produced by painting the design required in Japan gold size and pressing a sheet of transfer gold on to the tacky surface. Leaf will only adhere permanently to the tacky size.

GLASS
First of all it is important to differentiate between the various types of glass. There are two kinds of common or garden glass: soda glass and potash glass which are in the main used for household and domestic purposes. Other types have different properties and are employed in varying ways, differences being produced by the introduction of various chemicals into the raw materials used in glass production, resulting in heat-resistant glass, Crookes glass which inhibits the passage of ultra-violet light, unbreakable glass, etc. The introduction of metallic oxides into clear glass produces various transparent and translucent colours (hence, for instance, bottle glass and cranberry glass), and one colour glass can be overlaid on another to produce artistic effects. Glass is blown and moulded, or pressed, to form various shapes. It can be cut and polished, etched, sand-blasted when at normal temperatures, and moulded when heated. None of the manufactured glasses should be confused with rock crystal, which is a natural material found in different parts of the world and much prized by ancient cultures for the fashioning of jewellery and religious artefacts.

Crystal glass contains various proportions of lead which is introduced to make it sparkle – but it also makes it brittle, so that it chips and shatters very easily. Best lead crystal contains 24 per cent lead, reflects all the colours of the rainbow when correctly cut, and has a pure metallic ring. It is, of course, used for making cut glass and chandeliers and is called lead crystal. When glass is merely described as crystal, or crystalline, or indeed by any other name, it is of inferior quality and contains less lead.

Because nearly all glass is brittle and easily broken – the better the quality, the more fragile it becomes – take great care when cleaning it. Normally a washing in warm water containing a little detergent is sufficient, but when it has been exposed to grease, soot, tobacco smoke and other contaminating influences, stronger measures will be required. Do not use very hot water, for violent changes in temperature will cause some glass to crack. Allow the glass to drain, dry it with a soft tea-towel and then polish with a chamois leather. It is not advisable to wipe away dust without washing, as dry dust may contain sharp elements which can cause minute scratches. Persistent stains, such as hard water deposits, wine and chemical stains, need more severe treatment. First try washing in household ammonia which will make the article sparkle more brilliantly than washing in detergent. Spirits of salts (32% solution of hydrochloric acid) in a diluted form will remove lime and hard watermarks. A 5% Sulphuric 🔥 or Nitric 🔥 acid solution will remove most stains, but acids are somewhat dangerous to use and not readily available. One effective way of cleaning the interiors of narrow-necked vessels like decanters is to swill the inside with warm water and a denture cleaner such as Steradent.

Glass-bonding materials have recently been revolutionised by a new preparation: Cyanoacrylate Ester (see **adhesives**) – the most widely distributed form is Loctite Glass Bond – which produces an almost invisible join in nearly all glass. This unique adhesive uses the ultra-violet element in daylight to harden it. In strong sunlight, it dries hard in less than 10 seconds and, on a dull, cloudy day or in partial shade, takes up to two minutes. It will not dry in artificial light containing no ultra-violet rays. Make absolutely sure that the surfaces to be glued are clean, dry and close fitting. If in any doubt, swab them off with meths 🔥 or Acetone 🔥. First, shield the pieces from the light before applying the adhesive very sparingly to only one of the surfaces to be joined. Bring the two surfaces together, accurately positioned. Then expose to strong light. Excess glue can be wiped away with tissue moistened with meths 🔥 or

Acetone or when dry can be pared away with a sharp blade.

Minor chips can often be rubbed down with a fine Carborundum stone of the type used for sharpening chisels or with fine wet and dry Emery paper. Coarse abrasives will produce visible scratches which make the glass opaque, but polishing with a fine **abrasive** will remove these scratches. If you have a rotating polishing mop fitted to an electric drill, dressed with jeweller's rouge or Crocus powder, this will polish out all but the deepest scratches. But beware of letting the glass overheat. This treatment calls for caution.

GLASS STOPPERS
Ground glass stoppers often get stuck in bottles if they are left to stand for long periods. To prevent this happening, apply a smear of vaseline. When already stuck fast, first try warming the neck of the vessel, which will cause it to expand slightly. Then try heating the bottle gently to make the air inside expand to blow the stopper free. If this also fails, make up a solution of methylated spirit and glycerine (2 to 1) and add a few crystals of camphor (from the chemist). Irrigate the stopper with this solution for a few hours and then twist until it loosens.

HANDLES – see FURNITURE REPAIRS, FURNITURE POLISHING, BRASS AND COPPER FITTINGS

HARNESS – follow directions for LEATHER, BRASS AND COPPER, NICKEL

HINGES – see FURNITURE REPAIRS

HORN
Although not seen much these days, horn in one form or another was a versatile and useful material, used for such things as drinking vessels, gunpowder containers, lanterns, musical instruments, snuff boxes, adornments, and toiletry articles. As a result, at least a residue of horn articles has survived, many of them being of considerable interest and value. Some were mounted and embellished with silver, and have been venerated as ritualistic

symbols; in consequence, their preservation is of great importance.

Many kinds of horn can be softened and fashioned into the required shape by prolonged immersion in hot water, so wash in warm water using yellow household soap (not detergent), while taking care not to bend the horn unless you mean to! Dry the article immediately after wetting.

When the surface is dull and lifeless, it can be revived by burnishing with any metal polish. Follow this with a liberal application of wax polish. Where designs have been engraved on the surface, watch that the metal polish does not remove the colour that was used to fill in the design. If this has already happened, an application of coloured wax will often restore the detail. Just smear it all over and polish away the surplus. Horn is subject to flaking and cracking. For filling cracks, holes and splits, and to repair breaks, use Epoxy Resin **adhesives**. The glue can be coloured with pigment if necessary, to fill in small holes and splits. In cases of extreme deterioration, after repairing, give the article several coats of **varnish** – such as P.V.A. or Acrylic lacquer such as Furniglas P.U.15. This treatment holds it together and preserves it from further damage.

HORSE BRASSES – see BRASS AND COPPER

INDIA WORK – see LACQUERED ITEMS

INKSTAINS – see under item. Also FURNITURE CLEANING.

IRON
The two types of iron that are commonly encountered are cast iron, which is very brittle and will often break if dropped or carelessly handled, and wrought iron, which is malleable and used to make ornamental gates, screens and other architectural features. The traditional method of polishing cast iron stoves, fireplaces, and other domestic items was with blacklead which produced a polish and texture unobtainable by any other method. Once available from every ironmonger, you may have to search to find it. Reckitt & Colman* still make it as Zebrite. They will give you the name of

your nearest stockist.

Koldblack made by Jenolite Ltd and distributed by Frank W. Joel Ltd* chemically produces a layer of black iron oxide.

When exposed to moisture, unprotected iron artefacts readily rust, so have to be protected by painting or sealing from atmospheric dampness. Rusty iron can be cleaned up in a variety of ways. First remove all loose rust and scale with a wire brush, then apply a remover/inhibitor such as Jenolite (**rust remover**) to the manufacturer's instructions. Jenolite RRPL or RRPJ (Jelly) also leaves a coating of inert iron phosphate which is a positive corrosion inhibitor.

After cleaning and de-rusting, a protective coat is essential, even for articles kept indoors. A coating of light machine oil will give this protection, but its drawbacks are that it needs frequent renewal and it never dries. Wax polish is a good finish for antique ironwork where a natural look is desired. Otherwise a coat of clear lacquer, such as Rustin's Transparent Lacquer, or Joy Transparent Paint. A pleasing finish is also obtained with a matt black paint.

Broken cast iron can only be welded by a good blacksmith or welder, but you can do small repairs yourself with an Epoxy Resin **adhesive**. If there is any strain on the join, back it with a reinforcing layer of fibreglass. Fibreglass kits for motorists are obtainable from most garages and motorists' shops. Fibreglass and Epoxy Resins are also used to replace missing parts by using a cold-casting technique. Epoxy Resin casting materials, metal fillers and all accessories are easily available, see **Casting**.

IVORY

Before the introduction of plastics, ivory was an important raw material for the manufacture of a huge number of objects, such as knife and umbrella handles, toilet articles, billiard balls, piano keys, and figurines. It was a favourite base for miniaturists, and much used for decorative inlays. Right into the 1930s as much as 100 tons of African ivory a year passed through the Ivory Rooms in the London and Antwerp docks alone.

Strictly speaking ivory is the tusk of elephants, but walrus and whale teeth are also classed as ivory; it is difficult to differentiate

between the various teeth once they have been carved. Due to its
high cost, large numbers of imitation ivory articles appear on the
market from time to time and some are deliberate fakes. Just
recently scrimshaws (carved whale teeth), identical copies of
silver-mounted carvings of ships and nautical designs, have been
circulating; made of plastic, these are so realistic that even experts
are taken in.

In the early 1920s inexpensive copies of Art Deco figurines were
made of Spelter instead of Bronze, and Ivorine (an early plastic)
was used instead of ivory for the hands and faces. While these are
certainly collectors' pieces, they are nowhere as valuable as those
modelled by such masters as Franz Preiss, for instance. Many
oriental carvings are artificially coloured in a variety of shades; old
ivory which has been packed away where the light cannot get to it
yellows naturally. Exposed to extreme temperatures ivory will split
and crack. Exposure to wet will cause warping and distortion, but
short periods of wetting during the cleaning will cause no damage if
the article is thoroughly dried afterwards.

The easiest way to whiten ivory is to coat it with a stiff paste made
of china clay wetted with 20 vols. strength of Peroxide of Hydrogen.
Let the paste dry and then gently brush off. It is always advisable to
consult an expert before touching valuable antique ivories. Do not,
for instance, attempt to clean antique ivories which have been
shaded by the carver to highlight certain features.

Repairs to broken pieces are normally quite simple, as ivory
breaks clean. Epoxy Resin **adhesives** or P.V.A. make a virtually
invisible repair. Protect ivory pieces by giving them an occasional
polish with Micro-crystalline wax. Some authorities also
recommend almond oil.

JADE
Although most people associate jade with a distinctive translucent
shade of green, this type of stone can assume many different
colours, ranging from near white, pink and yellow to greenish black.
Like marble, jade often has streaks of varying shades running
through it. In fact, two similar minerals, jadeite and nephrite are
classed as jade. Jadeite is more translucent and is usually a deeper

emerald green; nephrite covers a wider range of colours and, when polished, has a soapy appearance.

Like so many other natural materials, imitations appear on the market from time to time, but real jade is distinguishable by its characteristic coldness and hardness – it will even scratch glass. It is, of course, a carving stone much favoured by Chinese craftsmen, so oriental subjects predominate, but untypical examples may be of Indian origin where it is also a traditional material. Clean jade by washing it in soapy water.

Repairs can be effected with Epoxy Resin or Cyanoacrylate Ester **adhesives**. Epoxy Resins, suitably coloured with powder pigments and a suitable filler, such as China Clay, can be used to fill cracks or model small missing features. Alternatively use an Epoxy Resin putty, such as Sylmasta, suitably coloured with pigment.

JAPANNED WARE – see LACQUERED ITEMS

JET

Whitby Jet jewellery, worn during mourning by our Victorian forebears, enjoyed a long vogue of popularity during the last century. It was also used for the manufacture of a whole range of trinkets and souvenirs. It is lignite, a type of coal that can be carved and polished to sparkle when treated in similar fashion to gemstones. It should not be confused with black glass which was also used for similar purposes.

Clean by rubbing with a cotton-wool swab moistened with soapy water. Dry and polish with a soft duster. For repairing breaks, use Epoxy Resin or Cyanoacrylate Ester **adhesives**.

JEWELLERY

It is obviously necessary to differentiate between precious metal and gemstone jewellery as opposed to the costume variety. Today Victorian paste, costume and semi-precious jewellery is much collected and in consequence is assuming a greatly enhanced value. Amber, coral, crystal, cut steel, diamanté, enamelled, filigree, jet and porcelain jewellery have all enjoyed their vogue and all are now collected.

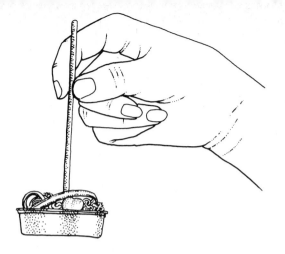

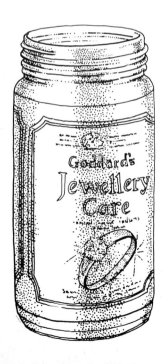

Cleaning a delicate piece of jewellery using Goddard's Jewellery Care and dipping basket.

All jewellery needs cleaning from time to time, to remove the accumulated deposits of dirt, dust, body oils, etc. which make it look dull and lifeless. The most effective general method is to use a proprietary product like Goddard's Jewellery Care. Merely dip the jewellery in the solution and soak for two minutes, brush the article with the brush supplied to remove any embedded dirt, and polish dry with a soft clean cloth.

As an alternative, household ammonia is a safe and effective solvent which can be similarly used to make both precious and costume jewellery sparkle. But be careful of the fumes.

Some gems require special attention. Pearls, for example, should never be washed, but worn as often as possible as the natural skin oils enhance their lustre. Extra care should be taken with emeralds too, as they are brittle and chip easily. Opaque stones are normally porous, so opals, turquoise etc should not be wetted, but only polished with a soft chamois leather. Marcasite jewellery should never be washed, just buffed up with a soft bristle brush. Always keep diamonds separate from other jewellery because they scratch the softer stones and metals. Repairs to valuable jewellery should be entrusted to a reputable jeweller. Cheaper costume jewellery can be refurbished at home and most handicraft shops carry a range of jewellery accessories, such as earring wires and clips. Detached stones are often glued into their mounts. To refix, use P.V.A. or Cyanoacrylate Ester **adhesives**. For this work use a pair of tweezers and a magnifying glass to ensure accuracy. It is not generally appreciated that metals can be stuck together with a modern fixative such as Epoxy Resin and Cyanoacrylate Ester. New pins and clasps can therefore be fitted in place of broken ones. Glass and other artificial stones and beads can be repaired with Loctite Glass Bond.

LACE

Decorative edgings to fabrics such as collars and cuffs, tablecloths and petticoats have been used as embellishments ever since Roman times. These laces have been produced either by plaiting threads together on a pillow where the pattern is marked out with pins (pillow lace), working with a single thread and needle or crochet hook (needle point), or pulling certain threads out of a woven fabric (drawn thread).

Very little lace earlier than the seventeenth century exists outside museums and most of it is of Low Countries or French origin. English lace dating from the late seventeenth century (Honiton and Buckingham) was influenced by Flemish patterns. Up to the beginning of the nineteenth century (1790–1800) the work was extremely fine and intricate, after that date the patterns became less complicated. Machine-made lace became increasingly common after 1820.

Antique lace which has become discoloured and yellow should be placed in the hands of an expert as the filaments often become so fragile that inexpert handling or the mildest of bleaching agents can result in damage. Under no circumstances use any form of household bleach.

Tack fragile pieces of lace securely to a backing of nylon net before soaking in distilled water. Several changes are advisable before introducing pure soapflakes to the bath, followed by several rinses in clean water. Avoid rubbing or scouring, confining any mechanical action to gentle squeezing. Always use the net backing to support the lace and dry it by pressing between layers of soft cloth or blotting paper. Never iron antique lace, just cold press it dry.

If repairs are needed, these should ideally be executed with the same type of thread as originally used; nothing looks worse than a repair in machine-produced cotton to a linen or silk specimen. Threads used for repairs can be coloured to match the work before use by either fading with strong bleach or colouring with a dye.

LACQUERED ITEMS

The process of lacquering consists of painting slightly raised figures and oriental scenes on a glossy background which may be black or crimson, less frequently green, cream and yellow. Gold leaf and paint were lavishly used in the decoration of long case clocks, chairs, bureaux, mirrors, cabinets, boxes and trinkets.

Such objects, sometimes known as Japanned or India work, were first imported into this country in the reign of Elizabeth I. They enjoyed great popularity during the reign of Charles II and there have been periodic revivals of this method of decoration throughout the history of furniture manufacture. The demand for it became so great that English craftsmen had to find ways and means of producing it domestically rather than importing ready-decorated panels in the form of screens from the Orient, mainly China. Methods of reproducing a lacquered finish were introduced to British workshops as early as 1688 and, as a result, some very odd 'oriental' scenes survive on home-produced lacquered furniture.

When dirt and wax has obscured the decoration, clean off by gentle application of white spirit on a soft rag. This will remove wax polish and dirt without attacking the varnish or French polish which may have been applied at some time during its history. If, after removal of the surface dirt, you find that the designs are still obscured by layers of discoloured varnish, this will be a job only for an expert restorer.

When washing down with white spirit, take care that the design is not damaged. English lacquer work was often executed on a GESSO base which may have cracked and flaked; its consolidation is also a task for the expert, but small chips and missing portions can be filled in and brought up to the correct height with a **filler** such as Polyfilla or Tetrion, and rubbed down to a smooth surface. To paint the new surface, use acrylic artists' colours as they are quick-drying and can be used fairly thickly to replace tiny chips. To restore gilding, see under GILDING (*Gold Leaf illumination*). Details can be painted on top of the layer of gold.

If, after cleaning or repairing, the surface is dull and lifeless, brighten with a clear **wax polish**. Alternatively, for protection and to consolidate the decoration, a single coat of clear French polish can be applied – see FURNITURE – FRENCH POLISHING.

LANTERN SLIDES
Slides for magic lanterns are normally 3 inches square and are either photographically produced or are transferred colour pictures – often hand-coloured, and in consequence not very securely fixed. The edges are often bound with passe-partout tape; sometimes this

holds together two sheets of glass with the picture between.

Brush away dirt and dust with a soft artist's brush. Before washing with either warm water or a solvent ensure that you only treat the glass surface, not the one to which the image is stuck.

Lantern slides are best stored in a special case with wooden separating slats to prevent the formation of Newton's Rings.

LEAD

This is a soft, heavy metal with a low melting point which lends itself to casting and beating into such items as garden figures, gutterings and ornamental rainwater hoppers. When first cast it is bright and silvery, but it soon weathers to a dull grey.

To clean, scrub with turpentine until the desired colour is achieved. When dry, maintain the colour by coating with **wax polish** and burnishing with a shoe brush or soft rag. It can also be sealed with a clear lacquer.

If you can get to the other side, push out dents with a rubber hammer (rather than a metal one which will leave marks). A good plumber will repair splits and holes.

LEAD CRYSTAL – see GLASS

LEAD SOLDIERS

These are now very collectable, but have usually been played with until most of the original paint has been chipped off. The value of repaints is much lower than of original examples, even if they are slightly damaged, so consult a specialist before repainting. Mended and repainted soldiers in their original liveries are, of course, attractive collectors' items. Any model shop will supply Humbrol enamels in small pots for renovating the paint.

LEATHER

Leather has been used to upholster furniture, to cover trunks and boxes and for a host of other uses back into the mists of time. With age, leather perishes and is also susceptible to rotting. All leathers which do not have a suede surface can be cleaned and fed with saddle soap, made by Properts and obtainable from any leather shop or saddler.

Delicate antique leathers, such as book bindings and box coverings should be cleaned with British Museum Leather Dressing (see under **leather treatments**). The dressing is applied with a soft rag or cotton wool rubber and the article left for a day or so until the solution has penetrated and dried out. It can then be buffed and, if required a coat of good quality leather polish can be applied. Coloured polishes can of course be used to revive fading colours, but do not destroy the antiquity of anything by over-renovation. A good neutral preservative is Connollys Cee Bee Hide Food or Meltonian leather cream polish.

Where you have to deal with crumbling surfaces that are too far gone to be revived with Propert's Leather Soap, they can often be consolidated by a brush coat of colourless French Polish. Meltonian market a range of leather dyes that can be used for renewing faded colours or you can use aniline dyes in methylated spirit on the surface before applying the French Polish.

Suedes or other buffed finishes should be cleaned with proprietary suede cleaners according to makers instructions. These are more likely to be effective than using solvents such as Carbon Tetrachloride 🔥 .

Mending tears Stick a patch of new leather on to the back face, if it can be removed or otherwise got at. Weak or fragile pieces of leather can be reinforced by backing them with hessian or canvas. Use an acrylic adhesive for small repairs and a P.V.A. adhesive for larger ones (see **adhesives**). Where sewing is the only possible means of repair, use a shoemaker's thread and wax it before use, with either beeswax or a candle stub.

Table and desk tops As such leathers frequently need replacement it is best to buy them from the specialists firms who advertise in the antique press. Given the dimensions of a rectangular leather or an accurate paper pattern of irregular shapes, these companies will produce a leather to fit, complete with gold blocking and a 'blind edge' which is a tooled pattern without gold around the perimeter of the leather. The leather will have a selvage

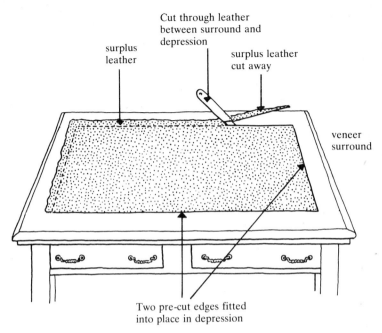

Recovering a leather desk top

on it when it comes, so to ensure that it fits as perfectly as possible, this must be cut off two adjoining sides, using a straight edge on rectangular leathers.

The surface of the table or desk must be prepared by removing every vestige of old covering and glue. This is best done by wetting it and using a chisel scraper (as used to remove wallpaper).

Leather is easily stretched out of shape, so do not apply glue to the prepared leather, only to the surface where it is to lay. P.V.A. **adhesive** is the best to use but if a fairly large area has to be covered, wet the surface with water before spreading the glue with a comb-edged spreader. (These are supplied free with many adhesives and you can get one from any DIY shop). An alternative is to use a wallpaper adhesive, but these tend to be too wet and cause the leather to stretch and bubble.

Having glued the whole surface, take the leather and place the pre-cut corner in place and proceed to spread out the rest of the leather progressively over the surface, using a soft rag to exclude air bubbles and watching that the edges fit snugly up against the veneer border or excavated recess made for the leather to fit into. Minor re-adjustments are easily made as the leather will slip on the glue surface until it is firmly pressed down.

There will be an overlap of the selvage, and the leather will have to be pressed into the recess with a paper knife or similar blunt-edged tool. This will mark a line where the leather is to be cut to fit. Do this with a sharp knife, such as a Stanley Knife. It must be sharp and should be angled towards the rebate slightly. Start in the corner and take hold of the waste strip of leather in one hand pulling it away from the table top as the blade cuts it free. In this way, even if the blind edge doesn't quite fit, the leather will be exactly right and the small discrepancy will not show. This is better than trying to stretch or shrink the leather into exact shape.

Gold leaf borders are applied by transferring from a gold strip with a heated brass patterned wheel engraved with a continuous design.

LOCKED DRAWERS

Where no key exists, first assess how much damage you are prepared to risk to the woodwork and how much time and trouble can be taken over the operation. First try out all your old keys. Quite often the tongue of the lock is short enough for the drawer to be opened by easing the drawer-divider with a jemmy or broad-bladed chisel. Too heavy a hand will, of course, bruise or even splinter the surrounding woodwork.

If there is no point in locking the drawer once it has been opened, the tongue can be sawn off by inserting a hacksaw blade between the divider and the drawer itself. Take care not to damage the drawer. It can be protected sometimes by inserting a slip of veneer to prevent the blade from scratching.

Sometimes the screws securing the lock can be got at by removing the drawer above. If there is a drawer-divider obstructing access, it can often be withdrawn by taking off the back of the piece of furniture. Alternatively part of the divider can be cut away with a keyhole saw to facilitate removal of the lock. Or you can of course call in a locksmith to pick the lock with skeleton keys, but that will prove expensive.

LOCKS

Keys and locks tend to get separated, particularly on furniture when it changes hands. These days people do not seem so anxious to lock any but the most private drawers, but virtually all nineteenth and eighteenth century furniture was fitted with locks.

New keys can easily be cut for old locks by a competent locksmith, but you will have to take the lock to him. You will find that a single key is usually common to all the drawers in a chest of drawers or bureau, but the desk opening may have a different lock.

To clean neglected locks it is necessary to remove them and, if fitted with a shield, to remove this also. Good quality locks are assembled with screws, cheap ones have the shields riveted on, so the rivet head will have to be filed off. After all the dust and fluff has been removed, soak them in paraffin, white spirit or a patent penetrating oil like Plus Gas. If you decide to remove all the springs and wards, lay them out in the order you removed them so that they are easily identified for re-assembly. This is only necessary if you are a collector and wish to burnish up all the parts. Normally a gentle rub over with an old tooth brush is sufficient for working locks. Dry off the lock and give it a coating of machine oil before refitting.

MAHOGANY – see FURNITURE

MARBLE

Marble is a type of limestone that is easily sawn and carved, much favoured by sculptors and builders alike for its adaptability. It can be pure white, or varicoloured due to the introduction of mineral salts at the time of formation.

White and pale-coloured marbles are prone to discoloration, mainly caused by settlement of dust which becomes embedded in the slightly porous surface. Regular dusting is therefore advisable, with an occasional washing with warm soapy water. Careful drying is essential when cleaning highly polished marble kept away from the weather.

Where more thorough cleaning is required, use Bell 1967 Cleaner (made by Bell & Co Ltd) see **Stone Treatments**. Alternatively, use a non-caustic **paint stripper** and wash down thoroughly after the stains have gone.

To polish freshly cleaned marble use Bell Marble Polish or Microcrystalline **wax polish**. Test very white marble on a small corner before application, as yellowing may result. Another method of whitening and polishing at the same time is to make up a paste with water and French chalk and rub it into the surface until it is dry and burnished. This treatment helps to conceal deep-seated stains that have resisted removal.

Marble can be repaired with Epoxy Resin **adhesive** and chips and holes can be filled with Epoxy Resin pastes made by mixing the adhesive with **filler**, such as kaolin, titanium oxide or pigment colours as appropriate. A useful ready made filler is Sylmasta which can also be tinted. Veining in various colours can be simulated to conceal repairs using acrylic artists' colours.

A protective coat can also be applied in suitable cases using Belsealer.

MARQUETRY
Marquetry is the art of combining together veneer shapes of various colours to form designs or pictures, an art form that reached its peak in the late eighteenth century. In order to achieve perfect results, several sheets of variously coloured veneers were glued together, interleaved with sheets of coarse 'sugar bag' paper. The design was then fretted out of the laminated sheets with a special saw and the various sheets separated and washed clean before assembly into the final form.

When complete, the picture was held together by sticking a sheet of paper to the face before gluing it permanently on to the body of the piece of furniture. Final details were drawn, burnt or coloured in with dyes.

Marquetry and inlaid furniture can be cleaned in the same way as ordinary furniture (see FURNITURE CLEANING). Wetting with either water or solvents for short periods will not dislodge the different elements. If some parts are loose, they should be carefully detached, cleaned of all old glue and stuck back into place. See also VENEERING.

Replace missing elements by new pieces of wood of suitable variety and colour. The correct colour can be achieved by applying a stain.

Make a paper pattern of the missing piece (see illustration p.99) by covering the area with a sheet of paper Sellotaped in place; lightly scribble over the surface of the missing area to produce an outline. Cut out the resulting pattern and stick it on to a suitable piece of veneer. Adjust to make a perfect fit by sanding the edges as necessary, and then glue (with any wood glue) into place. Where missing, add additional detail with Indian ink or felt-tip pens. But it is recommended you practise on another surface first!

MEDALS – see COINS

MILDEW – see under item

MILK PAINT – see FURNITURE – STRIPPING PAINT

MINIATURES
Miniatures are commonly painted on ivory or vellum, often with fugitive paints such as gouache, tempera or even watercolours. Professional restorers shy away from interfering with them, so the best advice is the keep them safely away from direct sunlight which may fade them; make sure they are protected by glass and when they show any signs of deterioration, take them to an expert for advice.

Some miniatures are painted on metal bases, usually copper, in enamel, but are usually on patch and snuff boxes.

See also ENAMELLED WARE.

MIRRORS

The first English mirrors produced in any quantity were made by Sir Robert Mansell who started a factory in 1615. The glass was produced by blowing cylinders, cutting them open and flattening and polishing the glass on a stone. Silvering was done with an amalgam of tinfoil and mercury.

In 1663 The Duke of Buckingham started his famous Vauxhall glass works to make mirror glass, though the size of sheet that could be made was limited. For this reason large pier mirrors of the period were made up with several pieces joined together and often produced a distorted reflection. Silvering with silver, which gives a brighter image was also perfected during the late seventeenth century.

The conflict that often arises with antique mirrors is that the silvering deteriorates and they fail to produce a satisfactory reflection. In spite of the fact that the main value of mirrors lies in the frame rather than the glass, buyers tend to discount antique mirrors that have been resilvered. One solution is to remove the old glass from its frame and store it very carefully in a storage frame (old glass is extremely brittle and very thin) and replace it with a new mirror. This preserves the integrity of the article and also makes it usable. But, of course, a dealer will always inspect the back to see if it has been removed at any time.

Damp conditions accelerate the deterioration of the silvering of mirrors, so cleaning should be with a minimum of water or none at all. Rather use a proprietary window cleaner or methylated spirit on a soft rag. A final polish with old newspaper still seems to produce a brilliance greater than any other medium.

Resilvering or replacement is a task for an expert. Some glass and mirror companies will produce reproduction antique mirrors that do not give themselves away by being too bright. In London try Semnat Glass Works Ltd*.

MOTHER-OF-PEARL

Mother-of-pearl is the interior surface of seashells, and has a lustrous many-coloured surface. It was much used during the nineteenth century for decorating papier-mâché furniture, in

Victorian costume jewellery and for embellishing trinkets. It is a
relatively soft material that can be engraved and carved.

Clean with metal polish or fine **abrasives** made into a paste with a
few drops of water.

It is easily cut with a jeweller's piercing saw or fretsaw with a fine
blade and can also be filed and ground into shape for replacement
of missing parts. Use Epoxy Resin **adhesives** to glue replacement
pieces into place.

MOULDINGS – see BEADING AND STRINGING

MUSICAL BOXES
There are basically two kinds of musical box, those that employ a
pinned brass cylinder to play a tuned steel comb and those using an
embossed metal disc to do the same thing. They vary in size from
those that fit into snuff boxes to monster Polyphons over 6 ft. tall.
They were invented in Switzerland in 1796 and were popular
mechanical music-makers until superseded by the gramophone at
the turn of the century.

Cleaning musical boxes is a complicated business, best left to an
expert unless you are an experienced clock repairer. The two most
important things to ensure the well-being of a musical box are:
never let it stop in the middle of a tune, and never attempt to take it
to pieces without first letting down the spring.

The pins on a cylinder musical box are easily damaged; they may
get bent, they may even get broken off. The points of the comb can
also get broken as they are extremely brittle. When buying a box,
look first at these parts, as professional repairs are very expensive.
The replacement of parts of the clockwork mechanism are very
much easier and not so expensive. Underneath the comb, some of
the teeth are usually fitted with lead dampers and these can also
deteriorate. They become covered with a light grey powder and may
even stick together. Their replacement and the subsequent
re-tuning is also an expensive professional exercise.

Should you want to renovate a musical box yourself, the best
book is *Collecting Musical Boxes and How to Repair Them* by W.
Ord-Hume. (Allen and Unwin.) Application to one of the thriving

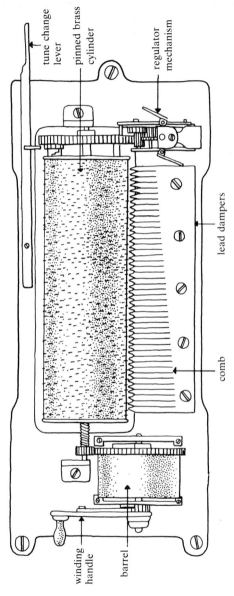

The inside of a typical musical box

Musical Box societies* will provide a list of specialist repairers.
Keith Harding Ltd* in London is one of them.

NICKEL

Nickel is a bright silver-coloured metal used in a variety of ways
from the minting of low value coins, to the plating of tablewares. It
is particularly useful as it takes a high polish and does not tarnish. It
was widely used for protective plating before the advent of
chromium, which has superseded it. It much more closely resembles
silver than chrome, though it does not have the brilliance and
sparkle of the precious metal. Cupro-nickel alloy is used for modern
British silver coins.

It responds immediately to silver cleaners. See SILVER. Scratches
can be buffed out with a fine abrasive.

NICKEL SILVER

When mixed with copper and zinc, nickel becomes an alloy known
as nickel silver, sometimes known as German silver. It is often used
as a base for silver-plated items and is marked EPNS (electroplated
nickel silver). Treat as silver when polishing. See also PLATED
WARE.

OAK – see FURNITURE

OIL PAINTINGS

Most oil paintings are not protected from the atmosphere by glass;
if they were, the surface reflection would detract from the
enjoyment of the picture. As a result, oil paintings are prone to
atmospheric dust which should be removed by frequent light
dusting. Oil paintings should never be hung over a fireplace in use,
not even over a gas or electric fire, as these produce convection
currents that increase dust circulation, and the sudden changes of
temperature are detrimental.

Oil paintings are usually executed on canvas stretched on a frame,
but may also be found on wood panels, ivory, metal sheets or even
man-made materials such as hardboard. The hardness, stability, and
reaction to cleaning materials varies from picture to picture, and

cleaning and renovation is a specialist undertaking if the work is of any great value. But there is no reason why many other paintings of lesser value should not be cleaned by the amateur. But do make sure that you are not tampering with a minor masterpiece.

Although beyond the scope of the amateur restorer, it will help you to know exactly what a professional restorer does to a picture. First the old, often discoloured or cracked varnish is removed, revealing the true colouring of the work. Holes, rips and other physical damage are repaired, and missing detail restored. Faded colours and lost backgrounds are revived, and sagging canvases tightened up. If the canvas is weak and liable to tear, the picture is removed from its stretcher and re-lined by adhering it to a new piece of stouter canvas. Flaking paint and bubbles are ironed back and, if essential, the whole work can be transferred on to a more stable and permanent base.

For the less valuable pictures, Winsor & Newton Ltd make Winton Picture Cleaner (available at any good art shop – if not, write direct to Winsor & Newton). If used to the instructions, it will clean off accumulated dirt and remove some old varnish. If you want added protection, revarnish after cleaning, using one of the modern synthetic Artists' Picture Varnishes which are applied either by brushing on, or with an aerosol. The proprietor of your nearest art shop should be able to advise you on this score.

You can try Acetone 🔥 surgical spirit 🔥 , ammonia or even Flash, but beware these drastic measures do not remove the picture, or at least some vital detail.

If the canvas is slack, it can be tightened up by giving the small wooden wedges in the corners of the stretcher a tap with a hammer. Tap the wedges in rotation to keep the tension on the canvas equal in all directions.

ONYX
Onyx is a kind of agate, a varicoloured stone much used for table tops and ornaments such as table lamps. Certain varieties are used for the cutting of cameos, where the design or picture is cut through the opaque white layer to reveal a more translucent and contrasting colour below. The commonest variety of onyx seen in Europe is that

with a predominantly green hue.

Clean in warm soapy water. Having a porous surface, it will absorb grease and stain marks. Remove surface stains by polishing with a cloth impregnated with methylated spirit, but wipe off spills immediately or they will penetrate.

Epoxy Resin **adhesives**, such as Araldite, are suitable for effecting repairs, and small holes can be filled with a putty made of an epoxy resin and a coloured filler, such as china clay or kaolin tinted with artist's powder pigments.

OPALS – see JEWELLERY

ORMOLU

Translated literally from the French, ormolu means 'gold ground up'. It is a term which is loosely used to describe bronze or other metal castings which have been gilded and applied as decoration to furniture, clocks and other articles.

Always remove ormolu decoration before attempting to clean it. Examination will reveal that it is easily detached by removing the small brass screws or dome-headed pins that hold it in place. Where pins are encountered, ease the casting loose using a thin bladed tool such as a small chisel scraper.

On much ormolu the gold surfacing may have partially worn away or otherwise deteriorated. It is, however, better to leave such areas as they are, rather than attempt to touch up. Depending on how much the surface has deteriorated and what the base metal is, clean by washing in a weak ammonia solution, using a nail brush or similar. Clean each piece separately. Transfer immediately into a bath of clean water. If this is not done, black stains impossible to remove will result.

Gold plated ormolu can be brightened up with a 2%–3% solution of Nitric Acid, applied carefully and immediately washed off. Nitric Acid, even in weak solution, is highly corrosive and must be handled with great care.

A safer and easier cleaning solution is Horolene which you will have to get from a clock repairer or supplier of clockmakers' sundries. Immerse the decorations in the recommended solution and work over the surface with a soft brush. Leave to soak for 10 to 15 minutes. Then plunge immediately into a bath of water and dry off.

A cleaner you can make yourself is also very effective:

> Sodium Hydroxide 1 oz
> Sodium Potassium Tartrate 3 oz
> Water 1 quart

Use as above. Both treatments will bring gold-plated and brass mountings up to showroom condition.

Occasionally you will come across ormolu that has been lacquered, and the old lacquer will have to be removed. The best material to use is a specially formulated solution from a metal finisher. **Lacquer remover** made by T.A. Hutchinson Ltd* is ideal. Alternatively solvents such as Acetone 🔥 and Amyl Acetate 🔥 can be tried, but with them you may find it a long job calling for considerable patience.

Ormolu can, of course, be sent to a plater for renewal of the gold, but it will look very new and bright. Antique furniture tends to look its best with the brass or bronze showing through. Over-restoration can all too easily look like reproduction!

PAPER
Most printing on paper, whether of pictures or writing, is with oil-bound inks which are fast to water and to most solvents; but, before employing any cleaning method, test a small area to make sure that the ink will not run. Some prints are coloured with water-colour washes which will immediately lift and run if wetted; others are signed in soluble ink by the artist and the signature could be lost if not tested before wetting.

Old paper is vulnerable to attack by fungus or mildew, which produces brown stains and blotches known as 'foxing'. They are removed by bleaching out. If there are only a few stains, spot treatment will suffice. Very often ordinary household bleaches are effective, such as Brobat or Milton, the latter being particularly so. Start off with a diluted solution and use a soft artist's water-colour brush to treat the areas of the spotting. It is always best to support the piece of paper on a sheet of glass, which allows the sheet to dry out absolutely flat.

Where widespread foxing is encountered, soak the whole sheet for a few minutes. A plastic tray is ideal for this. While most paper will not disintegrate when wetted, it is unlikely to have much wet strength, so will need supporting (on the sheet of glass, again). Sometimes just soaking in several baths of distilled water will remove stains, but not foxing; and therefore, when the paper is thoroughly wetted, replace the water with a bleaching solution.

A safe alternative to household bleaches is Chloramine T powder, stocked by chemists. 1 oz in a quart of water should be strong enough. An alternative is first to wet the paper in a solution of chloride of lime ($\frac{1}{4}$–$\frac{1}{2}$ oz to 1 quart of distilled water), then transfer to a bath of diluted Hydrochloric acid (1 fl.oz per quart of water). When the foxing has faded, wash thoroughly in a bath of clean water.

Dry by placing several sheets of clean white blotting paper over the paper to mop up most of the water; then replace with fresh dry blotting paper and hold flat, still on the sheet of glass, and cover the whole area of the cleaned sheet with a sheet of hardboard with books on top. Ensure that the pressure is even.

Oil and grease stains can be removed with spot treatments using **solvents** such as Carbon Tetrachloride or Benzene ♨ applied with an artist's water-colour brush. Remove the solution of grease and solvent with blotting-paper and repeat several times. When nearly dry, place several sheets of white blotting paper both above and below the sheet and apply very gentle heat with a household electric iron.

Ink stains (but not Biro stains), are best removed by spot treatment with a solution of **Oxalic acid** ♨ (1 teaspoon in a pint of warm water) followed by thorough washing with distilled water, but be cautious as Oxalic Acid will take the colour out of printing ink as well as writing ink. As an alternative, also first to be tested, use 1 oz. Citric acid and 2 oz. Borax in $\frac{1}{2}$ pint of warm water. Tears and holes in paper can be mended by patching with acid free tissue-paper stuck to the back of the sheet with wallpaper paste, which contains a fungicide (most do). The fungicide is necessary because it is bookbinder's paste which most readily attracts fungus attacks. Where sheets are fragile or so badly torn that they need backing completely, do not use paste, which will cause stretching and distortion, but an artist's mounting material, such as COW gum. This is best applied in a thin layer using the edge of a piece of stiff card as a spreader.

PAPIER MACHE

Most papier-mâché furniture and accessories date from mid-Victorian times, although the process was used as far back as 1763, when one Peter Babel of Long Acre was employing it to manufacture picture frames. Papier-mâché objects are normally of black background, highly decorated with designs, often of flowers or fruit, and inlaid with mother-of-pearl. Papier mâché is much like lacquer work, but can easily be distinguished on close examination.

As its name suggests, papier mâché is paper mashed up with water to which has been added glue and a filler such as china clay. It was either pressed into shapes like tea trays and piecrust table tops or coated over wooden frames to make decorated furniture such as occasional chairs, needlework boxes, etc. The process facilitated the embedding of ornamentation such as mother-of-pearl and, when sanded down to a smooth surface and lacquered, provided an attractive base for painting and gold lining.

Papier-mâché articles often become excessively dirty due to an accumulation of polish and grime occasioned by a fear that any attempt to clean the surface would damage the painted design. In fact, cleaning can tremendously enhance the appeal of dull, grubby pieces. Care must obviously be taken to preserve surface painting but careful de-waxing with white spirit on a cotton-wool pad is unlikely to lift the artwork. Old varnish, too, destroys the brilliance of the mother-of-pearl inlay, and can be removed with fine wire wool impregnated with white spirit.

After cleaning, the surface may have become matt. If so, apply a single coat of clear **French polish** with a pad, or a coat of clear **lacquer** such as Furniglas P.U. 15. When dry, apply a liberal coat of good quality furniture wax polish.

Repair cracks and missing pieces with a **filler** such as Brummer or Polyfilla. When dry, sand flat the surface and paint with a matt paint to match the rest of the background; this will call for some careful colour mixing, as blacks are not easy to match. Restore the gloss by applying a coat of clear varnish.

For the replacement of mother-of-pearl pieces, cut them to size and stick into place with Epoxy Resin **adhesive**. See MOTHER-OF-PEARL. It is better to adjust the height of the shell piece by grinding away the back, but if the cavity is too shallow, this can be excavated.

PARCHMENT

Parchment (vellum is a superior variety of the same thing) was manufactured from sheep, calf and other animal skins. The skins were cured and treated with chalk, smoothed with pumice and sliced to produce sheets suitable for writing. During the middle ages and until the start of paper manufacturing in the fifteenth century parchment was the only writing surface available in Europe.

It is extremely durable if kept dry and was until the beginning of this century much used for legal documents. These were normally folded, and flattening and removing the creases is not easy as any damping will result in distortion and stretching unless great care is exerted and the sheets are kept flat with weights until dry.

First test to make sure that inks or colours will not run. It is sensible to fix the ink with an acrylic spray fixative obtainable from art shops. Then relax the parchment, either in the steam of a kettle or by pressing between sheets of damp white blotting paper; dry flat on a sheet of glass sprinkled with French chalk; hold the sheet flat by pressing several sheets of dry blotting paper on the top with suitable weights. Books placed on a sheet of hardboard or plywood will ensure even pressure.

Valuable manuscripts, illuminations and the like should only be restored by an expert.

PASTELS – see WATER COLOURS

PEARLS – see JEWELLERY

PEWTER

Pewter is an alloy of 85% to 90% tin, with added copper and antimony. In France up to 18% adulteration with lead was permitted and undoubtedly some antique British pewter contains an element of lead. From medieval times the various Pewterers' Guilds controlled the craft and 'touchmarks', similar to the hallmarks of silver, are often found on pewter articles, both of British and Continental origin. These marks are by no means always present and this does not detract from the value of a good antique pewter article. Multiple marks are often found, as the owner as well as the maker used to impress their marks.

Of recent years, antique pewter has become highly collectable and this has led to the production of a huge volume of 'reproduction' antique vessels, many of them so well made as to be mistaken for the genuine article and sold as such. Great care has therefore to be exercised when buying antique pewter. Look particularly for sharp edges and for touchmarks that are either blurred because they have been cast or too sharp because they have been struck with new, sharp-edged tools.

With age, pewter acquires a beautiful deep patina, provided it is properly cared for and regularly handled. It can be burnished up to resemble silver or left dark and just lightly polished, according to the owner's personal preference.

The traditional method of polishing pewter was with pumice powder mixed with vegetable oil or animal fat, but this treatment is too harsh by far for antique articles, no matter how long they have been neglected. Normally a good proprietary metal polish will restore the shine without destroying the patination. Goddard's Glow and Long Term Brass and Copper Polish are ideal for antique or matt finishes, but Long Term Silver Foam should be used to maintain a gloss finish. Extremely dirty and corroded pieces should be totally immersed in paraffin oil (which is better than white spirit for this purpose) for anything from a few hours to several days. Next dry off with an old newspaper and wash in warm soapy water. If a brilliant shine is required, use metal polish.

An ammonia or washing soda bath will remove advanced oxidization, but this treatment will have to be watched closely, as prolonged exposure will damage the patina. Again follow by washing. If a high silver finish is desired, do not use harsh abrasives, rather try Jeweller's Rouge or Crocus powder wetted with salad oil. Even the finest grade of wire wool will produce fine scratches in the surface.

Finally, the surface shine can be preserved and the object's beauty enhanced by using a **wax polish**; it will give a medium-term protection at the same time.

If soldering is needed, call in a specialist. However, many minor repairs can be undertaken with an Epoxy Resin **adhesive**.

Small holes in vessels can be repaired with putty. Sometimes glass was used as a base for a pewter pot. If lost or broken, embed a new piece of glass – ensure it is carefully cut to size by using a paper pattern – in a thin layer of the recommended putty. Push a thin layer into the slot for the missing glass and place new glass within. Allow to dry; trim off excess putty.

Dents
Get a silversmith to push out any dents or other irregularities. Two good reference books are: *British Pewter for Pleasure and Investment* published by John Gifford and *English Pewter Touchmarks* by Radway Jackson (Foulsham).

PHOTOGRAPHS
Negatives Do not touch either glass or celluloid negatives as there is always danger of a deterioration – even from finger-marks. Take to a specialist.

Positives Most old photographs are printed on slow exposure papers. Sometimes the fixing agent is poor and they are often liable to fade on prolonged exposure to bright light. They can be re-photographed and this is the best course if they are of great value or interest. Again, consult a specialist photographer.

PINCHBECK
Pinchbeck (sometimes called poor man's gold) was first produced by one Christopher Pinchbeck. It is a yellow alloy made of five parts

copper and one part zinc, and was much used for making costume jewellery around the turn of the nineteenth century. It can easily be mistaken for gold by the unwary, particularly when used for making watch cases, but, of course, it does not carry a carat mark, and tends to turn dark. The best cleaner is Goddard's Jewellery Care, though it will not restore the shine to tarnished metal. For this, use Long Term Silver Foam.

PLASTER ORNAMENTS
Plaster ornaments are still being given away on fairgrounds, but these days they are usually crudely painted in garish colours. Before the era of plastics however, more tasteful plaster statues were produced and are still to be found more-or-less intact.

Some were finished by hot waxing which caused the wax to penetrate well into the plaster. This finish was also applied to Victorian and Edwardian models and busts of ancient Greek and Roman marbles and of contemporary personalities.

They are usually encrusted with dust and, superficially, look as if they are stone or marble figures. To find out if they are plaster, take a discreet scraping from the base: plaster is much softer than any stone and not greasy (as are wax coated models).

Surface dirt and grime can usually be removed with methylated spirit. This should be followed by a fresh coat of clear wax polish.

Repairs are best done with Plaster of Paris which can be used both as an adhesive and a filler. Where a larger part is to be put back in place it is best to insert one or more dowels. Missing parts can be moulded and left to dry for an hour or so. As the plaster is such a soft texture, finishing can be done with sandpaper and modelling files.

PLATED WARE (SHEFFIELD AND SILVER PLATE)
From an antique point of view, it is important to distinguish between Sheffield and Silver plate. The former was produced from the middle of the eighteenth to the middle of the nineteenth century by fusing a small piece (or billet) of silver on to a large billet of copper and rolling it out until the layer of silver was extremely thin. The bonded metals could then be fashioned into tea services,

candlesticks etc. As a result the edges of the sheets were not silver plated; the backs of the sheets became the insides of vessels and they too were often not plated, but tinned, like copper saucepans. This unique method of manufacture provides clues to the identification of genuine Sheffield Plate articles, and is one of the reasons why you should think carefully before having Sheffield articles replated.

Sheffield Plating was superseded by electro-plating, which covers the metal base with an electrically transferred coating of silver (or other metal, like rhodium, which does not tarnish). The plating takes place after the article is manufactured, therefore the coating of silver is distributed evenly over the surface. Electro-plating is sometimes found on copper-based articles, but more commonly on Brittania metal or Nickel Silver and are stamped E.P.B.M. or E.P.N.S. Early plated articles are not stamped or marked at all.

Silver plate tarnishes very easily, particularly when exposed to smoke from a fire or other gases which pollute the atmosphere; it is sensible to protect it by displaying it in a cabinet or keeping it wrapped up in acid-free tissue paper, or better still, its own custom-made impregnated cotton bag.

When cleaning plated items, remember that any polishing, no matter how carefully executed, will remove a little of the silver from the surface and so hasten the day when replating becomes necessary. Fortunately modern methods cut down wear and extend the time between polishing sessions. Proprietary cleaning agents fall into three groups: de-tarnishers, polishes, and polishes with long-term protection against tarnishing. One of the best de-tarnishers is sold under the name of Goddard's Silver Dip. This is fine for smaller items, but salvers and the like should be polished with Long Term Silver Foam or Long Term Silver Polish. These products which are applied in the usual manner incorporate a chemical tarnish barrier, totally harmless and invisible, which reduces the frequency of cleaning.

You can make your own silver polish with a base of French Chalk made into a paste by adding methylated spirit and ammonia. It is best to use cotton wool rather than a cloth to avoid minute scratching. A dip can be made by making a solution of washing soda in a plastic bowl and introducing a square of aluminium foil. Immerse completely the tarnished article and when the effervescence has stopped, wash the article in clean water and dry carefully.

Silver plate repairs should be left to an expert. Most electroplaters will undertake repairs.

PRINTS – see PAPER

RING MARKS – see FURNITURE CLEANING – RINGS AND STAINS

RUSHWORK
The only kind of rushwork that requires repairing or replacing is rush-seating in chairs. It is not easy to find anyone to undertake rushing these days, so you may have to do it yourself, but the technique is not difficult to master and, as it is taught in most schools, you may be able to get some basic help from a crafts teacher.

Your local Craft Supplier may not stock rushes but two sources are Deben Craftsmen* of Ipswich and Dryad Handicrafts* of Leicester.

First soak rushes for 24 hours to make them pliable, then twist them together, two or three at a time. As the seat progresses new rushes are introduced on the bottom side of the seat where ends will not show, thus forming a continuous rope as the seat is made. The only trick to master is the continuous twisting of the rushes into a skein of more-or-less uniform thickness. An alternative is to use seagrass (also from the above suppliers), which comes in a continuous cord already twisted and is much favoured in school handicraft classes. It too will make a durable and attractive seat.

If you have never done any reseating of chairs, it is best to find someone to give you a quick lesson as this is much better than trying to follow complicated written instructions and diagrams.

To clean rush seats, scrub them with detergent and warm water and leave to dry out of doors in the sun.

RUST – see IRON, TINWARE and **rust removers**

SCABBARDS – see WEAPONS

SCIENTIFIC INSTRUMENTS
Scientific instruments of great antiquity, such as astrolabes,
telescopes and strobes are of great value and should not be
interfered with, except by an expert. Most eighteenth- and
nineteenth-century instruments are made of a combination of metal
and wood – mostly brass and mahogany. Sets of surgical instruments
are, of course, steel and are often housed in fitted mahogany cases.

Brass is often coated with lacquer which deteriorates with time
and should be cleaned off. Use **lacquer remover** made by T.A.
Hutchinson Ltd*. To treat the wooden parts, see FURNITURE
CLEANING and FURNITURE REPAIRS; brass, see BRASS AND COPPER;
steel, see FIREARMS.

Optical lenses are sometimes 'bloomed', which is special
protective coating, and should be handled with caution. Cleaning
with a camel-hair brush to remove dust is all that an amateur should
undertake, as dismantling and reassembling may not be as easy as it
appears. A camera repairer may be willing to help you if you cannot
find an optical instrument-maker to do the renovation.

SCREENS
There are many types of screen, but it is the 'draught' screen which
presents several peculiar problems.

The wooden frames of screens, made from silk or other fabric,
often need renovating; the problem of protecting the material then
arises. The only safe way to protect it from stain, polish, etc., is by
masking it with polythene sheet, held in place with masking tape. If
the material is particularly delicate, heavy masking tape as used by
garages may be too tenacious, so use an 'easy-peel' tape; as a last
resort, pin the protective sheet to the fabric's surface. This is not
really satisfactory, as polish can leak under the edges, but it is better
than nothing.

Scrap and leather screens usually have canvas or leather hinges
which perish and tear away. Reinforce these by sticking a strong
tape (such as Copydex Strong Self-Adhesive Household Tape or
Tuff Tape) over the faulty hinge. (Most DIY shops stock both, or

write direct to Copydex Ltd*.) Apply the tape from top to bottom of the hinge: as it is 2 ins wide, it does not need trimming in most cases, and will make an acceptable edging to the screen. You can also extend it to 'frame' the whole screen if corners and edges are frayed. To smarten up the screen, reinforce the tape with brass-headed upholstery tacks. However, the adhesive is quite strong enough to hold on most surfaces.

Repair damaged scrap screens by sticking new scraps over tears. Most poster shops stock reproduction Victorian or Edwardian posters or postcards which can be cut up for new scraps that will blend in. Stick them on with wallpaper paste and, if they need 'antiquing', use a slightly coloured clear **varnish** that tones in with the rest of the screen. Most scrap screens have been varnished to protect the paper from wear and tear.

SCREWS

Screws that have become embedded in the work to hand can cause much delay and irritation. First try a drop or two of paraffin – a simple method and quite often successful. Hardware and DIY stores sell more sophisticated oils: Plus Gas or W.D. 40 come in aerosol cans and can be very useful.

Where screws have become rusted into wood or metal try heating the heads with the red hot tang of a file or other suitable iron. The heat first causes the screw to expand and the subsequent cooling causes the screw to contract away from the wood, hopefully freeing it.

With really obstinate screws it is worth grinding down an old screwdriver to get the maximum purchase without tearing the screw head. A burred screw becomes progressively more difficult to turn. Place your screwdriver in the slot of the screw and strike it smartly with a mallet, then work it to and fro. The pressure on the screwdriver can be increased by securing the handle tightly in a grip or clamp.

As a last resort you may have to drill the screw out completely, using a high speed metal drill. The resulting hole can usually be concealed to an acceptable extent by fitting a wooden plug of similar variety of timber.

SHEFFIELD PLATE – see PLATED WARE

SILVER
The genuineness and purity of all but English silver can only be determined by testing with Nitric acid. Make a small scratch deep enough to penetrate plating, and expose the underlying metal; put a drop of acid on to this scratch. A light-grey reaction denotes sterling quality; a dark-grey reaction indicates sub-sterling; while base metals show a greenish, fizzy reaction. After testing, wash the article in running water.

Solid silver tarnishes, just as does silver plate. Years of cleaning impart a bluish tinted, deep patina which is far more attractive than the white metallic glint of new silver. This patina is to be preserved, as it adds both warmth and charm. Long-term silver polishes, such as those in the Goddard's range are excellent as they give extended protection against tarnishing.

Silver repairs should be left to an expert. Most electro-platers will undertake them.

SILVERING – see MIRRORS

SILVER PLATE – see SILVER and PLATED WARE

SMOKE (EFFECTS OF) – see OIL PAINTING, FABRICS

STAMPS
Stamps have always been a popular collectors item and both used and 'mint' examples are collectable. The more perfect the example, the higher it's value with a premium added for examples attached to selvages which bear printers' register and colour guides, sheet numbers and 'gutters' or unprinted areas which run down the middles of sheets of stamps.

Stamp collectors will look for examples of stamps in undamaged condition, used ones with good clean strikes of the franking stamp, unused examples in perfect condition and unmounted. Any stamp which has a mistake in the printing will assume additional value.

If stamps are collected as a hedge against inflation rather than a hobby, great care must be taken and reliable advice sought, as the rapid increase in demand had produced a crop of dealers of doubtful character, who indulge in all sorts of deceitful practices, such as regumming stamps that have been mounted and creating faults in order to take advantage of the unsuspecting investor.

There is nothing that can be done to clean or renovate stamps, other than soak used examples off envelopes in a tray of lukewarm water, and dry them, gum side up on sheets of blotting paper.

STATUES — see STONEWORK

STONEWORK
All stonework, whether hardstone such as granite and slate, or soft stone such as limestone needs cleaning and ridding of moss and lichen from time to time. The modern method of cleaning most exterior stone is to spray with clean water for as long as it takes to wash out the accumulated grime, perhaps up to two or three days. This, of course, is not always practical or possible, so other methods may have to be applied.

A. Bell & Co. Ltd* supply direct a range of cleaning and sealing materials specially designed for all kinds of stone cleaning. Suitable for cleaning slate, limestone, York stone, Muresque stone, reconstructed stones and red sandfaced bricks is Bell Special Marble Cleaner No. 7. Bell Oil Stain Remover No. 9 will act on oil and grease stains in all porous surfaces including concrete.

Belsealer No. 3 is a first-class sealant for all slightly porous surfaces and renders them impervious to oil, dust and dirt while bringing out to a remarkable degree the colour and patterns of the material.

Persistent moss and mildew can be removed and kept at bay by applying the fungicides available from builder's merchants for this purpose.

Broken pieces can be repaired with Epoxy Resin **adhesives**. Coat both surfaces with the adhesive and support them well while the glue is drying. Large repairs will require permanent internal support by dowelling with non-porous metal dowels held in place by a **filler** Epoxy Resin putty, such as Plastic Padding – which will take up the slack in the dowel holes (which should be drilled out with a masonry bit of suitable size). Cracks can also be filled with a plastic putty such as Sylmasta which is nearly white, and which can be tinted to blend in with the stonework.

STUFFED ANIMALS

Smaller specimens are normally found in glass cases and in consequence may have escaped the ravages of time to some extent. Larger heads for exhibition on walls are more vulnerable to attacks by insects and mites, and this will often cause the hair to fall out and the treated skin itself to start to disintegrate.

Do not remove or disturb the skin as it is difficult to get back into shape. Renovation should be confined to cleaning and, if required, disinfesting.

First of all remove all surface dust and dirt with a brush. On fur, use a fairly stiff one but, when dealing with feathers, take great care, as these can quite easily become detached. Use Fuller's earth (from any chemist) to remove more tenacious dirt. Dust on then brush away in the same direction as the fur or feathers lie.

For disinfestation, use any household **Insecticide**. Those in solution in spirit are better than dusting powders, as the residue is virtually invisible after the solvent had dispersed. Mites are more difficult to exterminate. If they persist, fumigation may well be the only answer. (Consult your Local Authority pest officer.)

When specimens are contained in glass cases, conceal mothproofing crystals in the case, as these provide long-term protection against silverfish and mites.

The insides of mouths, noses, paws, ears, etc. may require repainting or touching up. Use acrylic paints (obtainable in any art shop), as they are easy to mix and match, and dry quickly. Apply a coat of clear **varnish** where a gloss finish is required.

The refurbishing of the case itself is sometimes as important as the care of the specimen. Try to preserve the antique look of the case. Here again, acrylic paints lend themselves well, while dried grasses, etc., from a craft supplier, reinforce background settings. Use a plastic filler (as used in motor body repairs) to represent the ground and support grasses. Before it sets, sprinkle with sand and pebbles or, after hardening, paint to represent earth.

Sometimes you will need a new glass case. A builder's merchant will cut the glass to size. Fix the sheets together with a strong self-adhesive tape. Copydex make one in 2-in.-wide rolls. Cut the tape down the middle to 1-in widths.

STUMPWORK – see APPLIQUE

SWORDS – see WEAPONS

TAPESTRY – see FABRICS, WALL HANGINGS

TARNISHING – see SILVER, FABRICS

TEA CADDIES

Tea was an expensive beverage in the late seventeenth and early eighteenth centuries, costing as much as £2.50 for a pound of the best. Containers to hold it were therefore suitably grand to hold such a valuable commodity and were often both beautiful and lockable. They were called Tea Chests until the late eighteenth century when the word Caddy came into use. The word is a corruption of the Chinese word 'Kati', being a measure of weight just over one pound.

The interior was frequently divided into compartments to hold both green and black teas and often there was a third compartment to hold a mixing bowl, alas more often than not broken and discarded long since. The tea compartments were usually lined with tin or lead foil and this should be preserved, even if torn or otherwise damaged. It is not advisable, however, to attempt to reline them.

The exteriors are usually of exotic veneers, liberally embellished with inlays, stringing, cross-banding and brass fittings. The normal rules for furniture restoration apply, and there is great scope here as tea caddies are highly prized collectors' items.

TEAPOTS

Tea contains tannic acid, and it is substantially this material which causes the stain on the inside of teapots. It does not matter whether the teapot is ceramic or metal, a brown stain will appear with use. In extreme cases the stain will penetrate right through the china and discolour the outside of the pot.

Teapots therefore require regular cleaning if they are in constant use, and initial cleaning before being put on display. If you have some Borax in the house, fill the pot with warm water and add and dissolve a tablespoon of Borax. Leave it to stand for several hours. The inside can then be scoured out with a nylon or similar washing-up pad. The spout should be brushed thoroughly with a small bottle brush with a wire handle which will bend to fit into it.

There are also specially formulated products on the market which will remove stains from teapots, and most easily available being Stainfree and Chempro T, stocked by most chemists. Steradent denture cleaner can also be tried.

For repairs and renovations see the appropriate entries on BRITANNIA WARE, CERAMICS, PEWTER, SILVER.

Heat buffers

On some metal pots, a bone or wooden heat buffer is fitted to each end of the handle. Should one of them break and the teapot is in use, replacement must be undertaken by a professional craftsman, through a jeweller or electro-plating company. Show pots can sometimes be stuck together again with an **adhesive** such as Epoxy Resin or Cyanoacrylate Ester.

TEARS – see FABRICS, LEATHER, PAPER

TERRACOTTA

Terracotta is baked red clay and has been used for thousands of years to make a wide variety of objects from tiles, pots and urns to statues and architectural decoration. Normally terracotta is left in its natural red state, but it may be decorated by either painting or glazing, and some 'earthenware' crockery and kitchenware is usually glazed on interior surfaces.

When cleaning or repairing statues and other architectural features made from terracotta, follow procedures given under

STONEWORK. A paint stripper will remove most types of paint and varnish, also moss and lichen; for extended freedom from vegetable growth, see **fungicides**. Follow the treatment with a fresh coat of sealer if appropriate. But, for much external work, sealers are not aesthetically acceptable as they change the colour and texture of the original surface; to maintain the latter, regular cleaning is called for.

For small repairs, see CERAMICS

TINWARE

Antique household and kitchenware items made from tin plate are increasingly collected; when found, they are usually in need of thorough renovation. Very frequently, the coating of bright tin will have worn away in places and the duller steel body may have started to rust. The problem is to remove the rust and shine up the steel without destroying any more of the outer coating of tin.

Tin was widely used on kitchenware and for lining food containers because it affords protection from deterioration and does not rust or impart flavour to preserved foodstuffs. It was only superseded a few years ago when plastic and lacquer coatings were introduced into the canning industry. High-quality copper saucepans are still coated with tin on the interior surfaces.

First wash tin articles in hot water containing a little washing soda. Clean rusted edges and bare patches carefully with a fine **abrasive** powder taking care to preserve the remaining coating of tin as much as possible. Jenolite Jelly can be used to remove spots of rust. As moisture gets into folds and cracks where the tinsmith has made joins, place the article in a warm oven for a few minutes, to ensure that it is completely dry, and then polish with a wax polish.

TINWARE (JAPANNED)

Trays, tea caddies, spice boxes and suchlike were cheap imitations made to resemble papier mâché; plain lacquered tinplate was also made into deed boxes, trunks, hat boxes, etc. If in perfect condition, merely protect them with a coat of **wax polish**. Scratched or otherwise damaged lacquer embellishments can be retouched with acrylic paints. Polish when the paint has hardened.

TORTOISESHELL

Before the advent of plastics tortoiseshell was used to manufacture a multitude of small objects from patch boxes to combs. When heated it can be manipulated into a great variety of shapes as it becomes malleable. As it is naturally translucent, it was often stained with various coloured dyes or mounted on coloured backgrounds to enhance its natural beauty.

Clean tortoiseshell by washing with soap and water. Feed and polish with olive oil or beeswax polish. Like so many natural substances, tortoiseshell responds to handling and being used.

To remove blemishes rub vigorously with French chalk or talc on a cotton rag. Bad scratches are best left to an expert.

Missing pieces of shell are best replaced with **Hard Filling Wax**, which is similar to sealing wax and obtainable in a range of suitable colours from French Polish manufacturers. The technique is to heat the tang of a file (the pointed end that fits into the wooden handle) and let the wax dribble down it on to the area to be filled. Level the surface when the wax is dry, just a few seconds after melting, with the blade of a sharp chisel.

Remember, tortoiseshell can be spoilt by as little as one day's exposure to strong sunlight, which causes a chemical change in this material. It will become lustreless and cloudy – and no amount of polishing can cure the condition.

For tortoiseshell and brass inlay see BOULLE.

TUNBRIDGE WARE

As the name implies, this work originated in the Tunbridge Wells area, in the mid-seventeenth century, and was in constant production for over a hundred years. The technique involves the building up of pictures and designs using lengths of various coloured woods cut into square sections of about 1/16 in approx. After gluing together, thin slices were cut off and fixed to the surface of articles usually sold as seaside souvenirs, often boxes for stamps, cottons and the like. From 1827 to nearly the end of the century, large quantities were produced and are now much sought after.

Unfortunately, the varnish used to finish many earlier versions of these 'Presents from Brighton' is prone to deterioration and becomes opaque and discoloured, masking the fine detail of the design; it therefore has to be removed and replaced with a more durable protective coat. Take care not to disturb or detach the chequer-like sections of the marquetry design: quite often the old varnish can be removed by careful scraping with a sharp blade, but a **paint stripper**, brushed on and then removed with a ball of wire wool, is normally the best treatment.

When using the stripper, treat one surface at a time; take particular care to ensure that the design is securely glued to the body. Finally clean off with white spirit and gently sand down with fine garnet or flour paper before giving it two or three coats of varnish.

If large areas are missing, it is impractical to restore as original. Small missing areas can be filled with plastic wood or a suitably coloured wood stopper such as Brummer **filler**. Repair larger areas with a piece of light-coloured veneer (see VENEERS). Then sand flat with a fine **abrasive**. Colour in the design with a mapping pen and coloured inks or coloured biros.

However, the final varnish coat will alter the colour, so a test piece will have to be done to make sure that the colour balance is accurate.

TURQUOISE – see JEWELLERY

UPHOLSTERY – see FABRICS, LEATHER

VELLUM – see PARCHMENT

VELVET – see FABRICS

VENEERS – see FURNITURE REPAIRS – VENEER

WALL HANGINGS
When tapestries or other fabrics are hung up for decoration or display, it is important that they should not be strained or stretched; in nearly all cases it is best that they should only be attached by their top edge. It is also essential that they should hang at least an inch or

two away from the wall; this will facilitate free circulation of air and protect the hanging from possible damp and insect attack. Wall hangings, like all other fabrics, are vulnerable to ultra-violet light and should always be protected from bright sunlight to prevent fading.

The method of suspension is also important, the object being to distribute the weight as evenly as possible over the entire top border. Velcro strip (supplied by haberdashers) is the favourite but, if rings or hooks are used, make sure they are no more than 8 ins apart, even when tape is used.

Wall hangings are even more vulnerable to insect attack than carpets, so inspect carefully at regular intervals. See **insecticides**.

Moth-proofing should only be undertaken by a qualified expert. For stored hangings, however, protect them with camphor crystals.

WALNUT – see FURNITURE

WARPING – see BOOKS, FURNITURE REPAIRS

WATER COLOURS
Both water colour and pastel pictures are usually extremely delicate, the colours often being fugitive. If the picture in question is valuable cleaning and renovating is the work of a specialist. The use of any liquid, water or solvent based, may well cause damage – even fumigants can cause colours to fade.

India rubber may also erase the pencil lines which sometimes make up parts of such paintings. Fresh breadcrumbs rubbed gently over the surface will sometimes dislodge accumulated dirt, but watch for any deterioration of colours.

The gum used to consolidate both pastels and some water colours unfortunately attracts and encourages the growth of moulds. These can sometimes be removed with surgical spirit working carefully with a camel-hair water colour brush. 'Foxing' on unpainted areas can be treated with a mixture of one-third Peroxide of Hydrogen (100 vols if you can get it) and two-thirds alcohol 🔥 . Milton or other household bleaching agents, diluted to the manufacturer's recommendation, can also be used to remove stains, but always work on small areas at a time and hold a piece of blotting-paper in your free hand, ready to mop up excess liquid.

Pictures should be properly mounted behind glass in a card or other mount that prevents the work touching the glass and the backs of frames should be securely sealed with gummed paper to exclude dust. Self-adhesive tapes do not appear, in the main, to have the necessary long-term durability of gummed paper.

WAX ARTEFACTS

Throughout history man has used wax in one form or another, and many artefacts survive despite the impermanence of the material. Beeswax is the basis of most antique wax items, often mixed with other materials, such as tallow, chalk, hard vegetable waxes and, for the last century or so, paraffin wax.

In ancient Egypt, wax models were placed in the tombs of the Pharoahs; throughout the Middle Ages wax was used to cast official seals as marks of authority; in more recent imes it has been used to make artificial flowers and fruit, dolls heads, three-dimensional pictures and models of all kinds.

Even under glass domes wax articles can get dusty and the first process of cleaning is to brush the article carefully with a soft artist's brush. Blown air is more effective than trying to suck up dirt with a vacuum cleaner, but beware of too fierce a blast, it can blow bits off.

Remove tenacious dirt with a household detergent in warm soft water (rainwater will do if your tap water is hard) applied with an artist's brush. The colour of many wax models is contained only in the thin outer coating, so take care not to wash it away by too enthusiastic cleaning.

Repairs are best left to an expert as heating wax to soften it can easily result in complete collapse into a pool on the floor, and waxes need to be matched in hardness to produce satisfactory adhesion.

See also DOLLS.

WEAPONS

Weapons are almost always manufactured from steel, though sometimes other metals may be encountered, particularly where embellishments in the form of inlays are present. The main problem is therefore the removal and prevention of rust damage.

Many weapons are normally housed in a sheath, which may, in itself, be of particular interest and require careful cleaning and preservation. Sometimes freeing the blade from the sheath is difficult, particularly if the weapon has not been drawn for some time, and has got rusted in.

If the sheath or scabbard is leather covered, take care to protect it from the penetrating oil which must be introduced to the interior to release the blade. It may be necessary to allow a day or more where the sword is badly stuck. Hold the scabbard secure in a vice, protecting it from the steel jaws with softwood cushions, and gently tap the hilt with a rubber or plastic hammer. Sometimes it is easier to use a length of wood placed against the hilt as a punch, and tap the end of it with a hammer. The wooden punch must be moved around the hilt of the sword in order to apply the force evenly when attempting to free the blade.

Before starting work on cleaning the blade, see if it can be easily separated from the hilt. Part of the sword, called the tang, runs up through the handle and is secured at the top by either a screw or by burring (flattening) the end of the tang over a large bead or button. Often this burr can be filed away to release the whole hilt, which will then separate into its component parts, thus assisting the cleaning process.

Cleaning the blade requires care, especially if it is engraved or inlaid. Do not use power tools, but fine wire wool soaked in a mixture of light lubricating oil and paraffin. Alternatively, use one of the **rust removers**, such as Jenolite. Watch the blade carefully throughout the treatment to ensure that the action is not too violent and that the chemicals do not start to etch the metal. However, where weapons are badly attacked by rust and have been neglected for a long time, a balance has to be struck between removing the rust from the pitting, and damaging the original polish. It is undoubtedly best to remove as much rust as possible to retard any further deterioration.

Repolishing of steel parts is most safely achieved with the use of several grades of fine emery paper, starting with the relatively coarse and finishing with the fine. The use of a revolving linen mop driven by an electric drill produces quick results, but calls for considerable expertise, so practise first on something of little value before venturing to try your luck on a valuable piece of armour. The best mild abrasive polish to use, which will impart a shining, silver-like finish, is Pink Porthos.

To impart a real glint, the blade should be polished with a chain burnisher. This is a series of interlocking steel rings about 5 ins square on a leather backing. Rubbed over any steel surface, it will produce a finish unobtainable in any other way. Do not use a chain burnisher on shallow engraved surfaces or insecure inlays, as the treatment is violent and can damage fragile objects.

Hilts, handles and scabbards
These are made from a variety of materials, which should be identified before cleaning. Metal parts can be of silver, plated base metals or steel. Leather handles may be covering a wooden base. As with everything antique, it is always better to repair than to replace, even at the expense of the finished article looking less than perfect – indeed, fair wear and tear is an essential part of an article's antiquity. The replacement of badly damaged wooden, metal and leather handles and scabbards is not too taxing.

Handles of dress swords are often bound with 'gold' wire, and picture wire twisted or braided is the best replacement. Secure the ends by drilling a small hole in the hilt or handle; insert the ends of the wire into it. Glue in place with a quick-drying adhesive.

Scabbards are sometimes all metal, all leather, or a base covered with leather. Leather scabbards are relatively easy to re-cover. Thin leather of suitable size is first soaked in water to make it supple and easily stretched. Ease into place over the metal or wood base and sew along the edges with shoemakers' thread (from a shoe repairer). While it is still damp, leather may be embossed or tooled into patterns. Finally colour and polish with any proprietary shoe polish.

WEBBING see FURNITURE REPAIRS *Webbing*

WICKERWORK – see BASKETWORK

WOOD – SEE FURNITURE

WOODWORM – see FURNITURE REPAIRS and **Woodworm control**

YELLOWING – see under item and **Bleaching agents**

Section Two:
Cleaning and repairing materials and their uses

Contents

Contents

Contents

Abrasives
An abrasive is a substance for scratching, grinding and wearing down by rubbing. The coarser and harder the abrasive, the quicker the wearing down process and the deeper the scratches. The finer the abrasive, the finer the finish; indeed it is difficult to determine when abrasion stops and polishing begins. In fact, polishing is a mild form of abrasion.

Abrasives come in many forms: hard sharp particles adhered to paper, or incorporated into greasy bars or suspended in liquids, blocks, powders. They may also be formulated with corrosives and/or solvents for specific purposes.

Abrasive papers
Technology has advanced greatly in this area – quicker than information to all but the specialist user. *Sandpaper* is still widely sold in ironmongers, but it has been superseded by newer abrasives which do not wear out so quickly. These are widely available too. They are more expensive by the sheet, but cheaper in the long run.
AVAILABLE FROM: most ironmongers.

Carborundum/Emery paper
This, emery paper, or wet and dry paper are all varieties of paper or cloths coated with dark grey abrasive and are specificially used by the engineering trades and coach builders for rubbing down metal and cellulose painted surfaces.
USE FOR: smoothing and polishing all kinds of METALS.

Garnet paper
Like sandpaper, this is sold in several grades of coarseness, and you will need two or three grades from fairly coarse, for initial smoothing, to fine for finishing.
USE FOR: smoothing and polishing all kinds of WOOD.

Jeweller's emery paper
This is much finer than the engineering grades, and will produce a brilliant shine. It can be obtained in several grades, and the finest will produce a polish on iron and steel.

AVAILABLE FROM: Jewellers' suppliers, and some large ironmongers and tool merchants
USE FOR: GUN BARRELS, IRON, STEEL.

Lubrasil
This is a silicone lubricated paper that remains unclogged much longer than other varieties.
USE FOR: preparation for FURNITURE – FRENCH POLISHING

Wet and dry paper – see above under *Carborundum paper*.
USE FOR: rubbing down FILLERS

Abrasive powders
There are a number of grinding and polishing powders available, mainly but not exclusively used for metal finishing. They have various grades of fineness and coarseness. The principal ones are:
Carborundum powder
Crocus powder
Emery powder
Jeweller's rouge
Pumice
Rottenstone
Tripoli powder
Whiting.
AVAILABLE FROM: T.A. Hutchinson Ltd* in powder or bar form.
USE FOR: ALUMINIUM (fine grade); BRASS AND TORTOISESHELL (BOULLE) (use Pumice mixed with vaseline); CORAL (fine grade of Jeweller's rouge or Pumice); PEWTER (fine grade of Jeweller's rouge mixed with salad oil).

Abrasives: wire (steel) wool
This is one of the most useful and versatile abrasive materials, acting both as a scourer and burnisher. It is sold in eight grades: the coarsest being No. 4, the finest 0000. The best grades to buy are the coarsest and the finest, though No. 1 grade and 0 grade are the most commonly sold. Start with a coarse grade, and finish with a fine one. They can be used for both wood and metal finishing, either dry, or

in many cases with a lubricant such as White Spirit or machine oil, or with polishes or other chemicals. Wire wool is invaluable when removing old polish or paint from furniture, in which case you use it with a paint stripper. It can be used with Brasso or other metal polish for cleaning badly tarnished brass, or with soap or detergent for scouring many surfaces coated with stubborn dirt.

AVAILABLE FROM: most ironmongers for the commonly used grades; less commonly used grades from specialist suppliers such as Henry Flack Ltd* or Gedge & Co Ltd*.

USE FOR: BRASS INLAY AND STRINGING (use very fine 0000 or 000 combined with metal polish); removing old lacquer from CANEWORK (use coarse grade); FURNITURE, METALS

Adhesives
General rules

Many people seem to be convinced that glues do not work very well, or at best are unreliable. In consequence they tend to reinforce a glue joint with the additional use of such aids as nails, screws, brackets, and a variety of devices, all of which reduce rather than strengthen the repair.

Gluing is easy, provided you follow a few simple rules. Glued joints only fail when these simple, logical steps are not taken. *There are no short cuts*; it may take a little more time and trouble to follow them, but the result is success instead of failure.

Rule 1: You cannot stick fresh air together. Surfaces to be joined must come into close and intimate contact. Filling up a slack joint with an excess of glue will not make a durable repair. Maximum surface contact is essential if you want the join to be successful.

Rule 2: You cannot stick together dust, dirt, grease or perished glue. Old joints must be separated and cleaned thoroughly. Old glue can be scraped and scrubbed away with warm water. Grease can be removed with suitable solvents which must be left to dry out thoroughly.

Rule 3: Apply the glue to both surfaces unless otherwise instructed.

Rule 4: Once glued together, the joint should be cramped firmly and not disturbed until the glue has had time to set thoroughly. This interval will vary widely with different adhesives, but with non-quick-drying glues, joints should be left under pressure for at least twelve hours. Hardening time is also affected by temperature – the higher it is, the quicker the setting of the glue. Use artificial heat where possible to accelerate the drying time.

You can devise all kinds of ingenious methods of cramping – clothes' pegs, elastic bands, self-adhesive tape, strands of elastic material wound several times round the work, heavy weights – the possibilities are legion; but it is always wise to prepare your method of holding and cramping before you apply the glue.

Rule 5: Always remove excess glue as soon as possible.

No adhesives are suitable for every job, so refer to the following guide before starting. The instructions on manufacturers' containers are always helpful, but remember the manufacturer will always say what the glue *will* stick, but rarely what it *will not*.

Acrylic adhesives
These are usually supplied in tubes and are widely used by model makers as they are *quick acting*, setting as little as ten seconds, as much as twenty minutes. Setting time can be speeded up by applying heat with an electric pressing or soldering iron. These clear liquid glues are suitable for a wide variety of sticking jobs, and are applied direct from the tube in a thin layer to both surfaces to be joined. If the material is porous, apply two coats before bringing the surfaces together. Although waterproof and fairly durable, they can break down when exposed to frequent washing in hot water, but are ideal for repairing collectors' display items.
BEST KNOWN BRANDS: UHU, Bostik 1, Gloy Household adhesive.
AVAILABLE FROM: most stationers, model and DIY shops.
USE FOR: BASKETWORK, BONE, CANEWORK, CERAMICS, COSTUME JEWELLERY, DOLLS' HOUSES, GLASS, small repairs to LEATHER, PAPER, PARCHMENT, small repairs to VENEER and WOOD.

Carpenter's (or Scotch) glue
Until the advent of plastics, all glues were made from 'natural' materials, such as animal bones and skins, starch, fish offal and the sap of trees. These traditional materials were used in the

construction of all antique furniture, at least until the first World War. Carpenter's or Scotch glue should still be used for the repair of important antique furniture, where the employment of traditional materials is essential.

This glue has to be prepared in a water-jacketed gluepot, for if it is allowed to boil it will turn dark and stain the wood. These days it is only obtainable in pearl or jelly form. The pearls have to be soaked in cold water overnight to allow them to swell and soften. Ensure that there is a little surplus water in the bottom of the outer container, and heat the glue in the inner pot. The heated glue should be thin enough to run off the brush, the last drop returning to the brush. It is best if this type of glue can be applied to warmed wood in a pleasantly warm workshop. Allow up to 24 hours for drying.

AVAILABLE FROM: most good hardware and DIY shops, or direct from Gedge and Co Ltd*, W.S. Jenkins Ltd*.

USE FOR: ANTIQUE FURNITURE, FRAMES

Cyanoacrylate Ester

These are the newest, most effective, *fastest setting* and most expensive adhesives to come on the market. A single drop from a tiny tube will hold two pieces of metal together and, after one minute, the joint will support tremendous weights. These adhesives, because so little is required, make virtually invisible repairs to clean breaks in glass, ceramics and similar materials. In the case of Loctite Glass Bond, this unique adhesive uses the ultra-violet element in daylight to harden it. In strong sunlight it dries hard in less than ten seconds and on a dull, cloudy day or in partial shade takes up to two minutes. It will not dry in artificial light containing no ultra-violet rays.

Great care has to be taken to avoid skin contact, as the glue will weld fingers so firmly together that surgical aid could be required to separate them. However, the advantages of the material outweigh all the drawbacks if selectively used.

BEST KNOWN BRANDS: Loctite, Cyanolit 202.

AVAILABLE FROM: Many stationers and DIY shops, and ironmongers, or direct from Alec Tiranti Ltd*, Frank W Joel Ltd*

USE FOR: AMBER, BRASS, CAMEOS, CERAMICS, COPPER, CORAL, GLASS, JADE, JET, METALS (JEWELLERY).

Epoxy resins
Thes glues are supplied in twin tubes, one of adhesive, the other of hardener. They have to be mixed thoroughly before application. Two sorts are widely available, those taking about six to twelve hours to dry, and the *quick drying* varieties which will harden in about five minutes. They are suitable for mending a wide variety of items and will stick metals together providing they are thoroughly degreased and the surfaces roughened to provide a key. They are particularly useful for restoring ceramics, as they can be turned into a filling putty by the addition of kaolin or titanium oxide. They can also be coloured by the addition of powder colours. Small parts can also be modelled from the putty. They can mend stonework. By adding powder colours, you can produce a veining effect which will conceal breaks in coloured marbles. A test is advisable on porous stonework, and terracotta, to ensure discoloration does not occur.
BEST KNOWN BRANDS: Araldite, Araldite Rapid, Gloy Fast Set Epoxy.
OBTAINABLE FROM: most stationers, ironmongers and DIY shops.
USE FOR: ALABASTER, AMBER, BONE, BRASS, BRASS TO WOOD (BOULLE), CAMEOS, CERAMICS, COPPER, CORAL, HORN, IVORY, JADE, JET, JEWELLERY, MARBLE, METALS (JEWELLERY), MOTHER-OF-PEARL, ONYX, small repairs to PEWTER, STONEWORK, TORTOISESHELL.

Impact (or Contact) adhesives
These products are used for sticking together large flat areas, such as table-tops and wardrobe sides. Wood veneers and plastic sheeting can be most easily stuck to thicker wood with these. Coat both surfaces with a thin layer of the liquid (makers supply a suitable comb applicator). The two elements can then be brought together, taking care that they are accurately aligned, as once united they cannot be pulled apart or relocated. Complete adhesion is immediate.
BEST KNOWN BRANDS: Dunlop Contact Adhesive, Evostik Impact, Bostik 3.

AVAILABLE FROM: most hardware and DIY shops.
USE FOR: VENEERS, large areas of WOOD, PLASTIC SHEETING.

Latex
These adhesives are manufactured from the natural sap of the
rubber tree, and are used for sticking fabrics and upholstery. They
are not suitable for other purposes.
BEST KNOWN BRAND: Copydex
AVAILABLE FROM: Ironmongers, DIY shops.
USED FOR: FABRICS, UPHOLSTERY.

Pastes
These are traditionally starch-based, and a quite effective one can
be made with flour and water. Wallpaper pastes have recently
become more sophisticated, many of them being cellulose or plastic
based.
AVAILABLE FROM: DIY shops, wallpaper shops, ironmongers.
USE FOR: PAPER, LEATHER TOPS.

P.V.A. (Poly Vinyl Acetate) glues
These are the glues that have superseded carpenter's (or Scotch)
glue for woodworking. They are also suitable for mending
earthenware and other porous pottery. They are supplied as a white
emulsion, usually in flexible plastic bottles. P.V.A. adhesives are
not waterproof and behave in much the same way as a superior
Scotch glue. They are applied straight from the container to both
surfaces to be joined; the thinner the layer of glue, the more
effective it will be. Drying takes about four hours in normal room
temperatures, but joints should be cramped together for at least a
day to allow for maximum adhesion and full setting.
BEST KNOWN BRANDS: Evostik Resin 'W', Borden, Unibond.
AVAILABLE FROM: most ironmongers, DIY shops, and timber
merchants.
USE FOR: ALABASTER, BASKETWORK, DOLLS (COMPOSITION and
PLASTIC), DOLLS' HOUSES, EARTHENWARE, FRAMES, FURNITURE,
IVORY, JEWELLERY, LEATHER, VENEERS, WOODWORK.

Urea Formaldehyde adhesives
These glues usually come in powder form, some needing a catalytic hardener, supplied at the same time, sometimes incorporated in it, and only starting to work once the powder is wetted. They make extremely hard, firm joints which are nearly completely waterproof. When hard, unlike nearly all other adhesives, the glue has a strength of its own, and in consequence can be used for filling gaps and securing loose joints. Wherever possible however, it is always best to try to fill gaps in woodwork joints with slips of veneer or thin slivers of wood. Joints, once made, must be left cramped together for at least a day to allow for complete hardening. The glues have a 'pot life' of two to four hours, depending on the temperature of the room, so only make up as much as you want for immediate use. Before mixing, or before the addition of the hardener, they have an indefinite life.
BEST KNOWN BRANDS: Cascamite, Aerolite 306.
AVAILABLE FROM: good hardware shops and DIY shops.
USE FOR: BAMBOO, breaks in CHAIRLEGS, WOODWORK JOINTS

Bleaching agents
Natural bleaching occurs from exposure to ultra-violet light, but the process is slow, and chemical bleaches are therefore used. Two main methods are currently employed: the decolouring and oxidizing properties of Chlorine (used in most household bleaches), or oxygenated water (Hydrogen, Sodium or Barium Peroxide). The strength of these bleaches varies. Always start with the milder solution and work up to the strongest only after careful testing.
　The bleaches most commonly used in antique restoration are: Oxalic acid 🔥 , Peroxide of Hydrogen, and specialist bleaching preparations from polish and sundries' merchants. A full list is given below:

Acetic acid
White vinegar, in its best known form, will remove stains from prints, revive surfaces of furniture, brighten up coloured fabrics, and can be used to retain the patina on bronze.
AVAILABLE FROM: grocers as white vinegar; chemists as acetic acid.
USE FOR: BRONZE, FABRICS, FURNITURE, PAPER.

Ammonia
Ammonia is a gas, highly soluble in water and normally sold as a
solution. Household ammonia is a 10% solution, and the strongest
solution commercially available is known as Eight-Eighty
Ammonia, having 880 vol. of the gas dissolved in 1 vol. of water.

Until recently it was used as a chemical colourant of wood,
particularly mahogany. Today it is most commonly used to remove
grease and dirt from glass and china, and to remove milk and casein
paints from old furniture as these are impervious to most paint
strippers.

Ammonia, particularly in a concentrated solution, gives off
irritating fumes, and is best used in the open, or at least in a
well-ventilated room. Contact with the skin and eyes can be
harmful, so wear protective clothing when using it.
AVAILABLE FROM: chemists and ironmongers
USE FOR: CERAMICS, FURNITURE, GLASS, cleaning JEWELLERY

Chloramine T
This is a white powder which is most useful for bleaching paper, and
is used in a dilution of $\frac{1}{2}$ oz to 1 pint of soft water, made up just
before use.
AVAILABLE FROM: most chemists, Frank W. Joel Ltd*
USE FOR: PAPER.

Household bleaches
These are useful but not ideal for decolouring wood and whitening
really tough fabrics. *Never* use on delicate or antique fabrics as they
attack the material itself. They can also be used to remove foxing on
paper.
BEST KNOWN BRANDS: Brobat, Milton.
AVAILABLE FROM: Chemists, hardware stores.
USE FOR: FABRICS (tough only), FURNITURE, PAPER.

Oxalic acid
This is a strong and effective agent, sold in the form of white
crystals. But take care: it is poisonous! 🔥
The principal use of this chemical is the removal of ink and
similar stains from wood, and for decolouring stained timber. Make

it into a saturated solution by putting as much as will dissolve in hot water. The solution is then flooded onto the stained surface and scrubbed in with wire wool. The whole surface must be treated, otherwise you will run the risk of being left with a light patch where the ink stain used to be. Neutralise the area by thorough washing with clean water before setting aside to dry.

Oxalic acid will also remove rust, and other stains from fabrics and leather, but here should be used in a 50 per cent dilution – i.e. half water, half saturated solution; or one tablespoon of crystals to 1 pint of soft water.

AVAILABLE FROM: most chemists.
USE FOR: FABRICS, FURNITURE (INKSTAINS), LEATHER.

Peroxide of hydrogen
This is the most commonly used bleaching agent of the oxygenating variety. It is sold in varying strengths, the most common being 10 vol. (this refers to the quantity of free oxygen it produces) sold for medicinal purposes. Hairdressers use 20 vol. for bleaching hair; and 100 vol. is also commercially available. But the higher volume strengths only accelerate oxidization, and lesser strengths are safer to use on delicate materials. Its action on wood is speeded up by the addition of ammonia. But treat both liquids with caution, as their action on all kinds of things, including flesh, is quite dramatic.
AVAILABLE FROM: most chemists.
USE FOR: BASKETWORK, BONE, CERAMICS, ENAMELLED WARE, FABRICS, FURNITURE.

Sodium hypochlorite
This is a very efficient bleaching agent, but test before use.
AVAILABLE FROM: most chemists.
USE FOR: FABRICS, PAPER.

Wood bleaches
These are used commercially by the furniture and restoration trades, and are available from specialist suppliers. They will, when required, take all the colour out of most woods and remove even the most persistent of stains. They are to be used with great care,

following the suppliers' instructions closely. Best known brand:
Gedge's Original Ultrableach
AVAILABLE FROM: Gedge & Co Ltd*, Henry Flack*, W.S. Jenkins
& Co Ltd*.
USE FOR: FURNITURE.

Casting and casting materials
The technique of casting is useful when one requires to make one or
more replicas of parts of decoration: for instance, a detail on a
picture frame, which has been broken off or lost. However, a similar
area of the decoration must be available from which to make the
mould. If the part to be replaced is not too large, take an impression
with clay or plasticine, by pressing firmly over the section of the
detail you wish to repeat; then carefully remove it without undue
distortion taking place. Make the cast itself by pouring Plaster of
Paris, dental plaster or a similar medium into the mould. Make sure
that no air bubbles are trapped in the mould. When the plaster has
dried out, flatten the back to a suitable depth by a combination of
cutting and sandpapering. It is unlikely that the new cast will fit the
space for which it is intended, so its shape too will have to be
adjusted before it is stuck into place with a quick drying adhesive
such as UHU or Bostik 1.

Epoxy Resin casting materials
These can be extremely useful in renovating bronzes, stone figures,
picture frames and a host of other antiques.
AVAILABLE FROM: Alec Tiranti Ltd* and Strand Glassfibre Ltd*
who will also advise on procedures.
USE FOR: BRONZES, FRAMES, STONEWORK.

Vinamould
This special material is ideal for more sophisticated moulds and can
be used over and over again. It is a flexible compound that has to be
heated and poured over the part to be copied. It is suitable for
casting in a wide variety of materials, and, because it is flexible, can
be used to cast pieces that have undercut areas which could not be
released from a rigid mould. When finished with, old moulds can be

melted down and used time and time again.
AVAILABLE FROM: some artists' suppliers, or direct from Alec
Tiranti Ltd*, Frank W. Joel Ltd*

Chain burnishers
These are squares of chainmail the size of the palm of the hand,
attached to a leather backing. They are extremely useful for
producing the finish on iron and steel implements, and are also used
for 'distressing' and burnishing old oak furniture.
AVAILABLE FROM: T. Marten & Sons Ltd*.
USE FOR: IRON, STEEL, OLD OAK.

Colouring agents
Acrylic paints
The newest range of artists' materials with a plastic base, made by
all leading Artists' Colourists under their own trade names.
AVAILABLE FROM: artists' suppliers.
USE FOR: all kinds of touching up and tinting in.

Black lead
For blackening and polishing iron artefacts
BEST KNOWN BRAND: Zebrite.
AVAILABLE FROM: ironmongers, or in case of difficulty write to
Reckitt & Colman.
USE FOR: CAST IRON.

Enamel paints
These are very high gloss oil paints, not to be confused with
enamelling glazes. You apply them by brush and they dry in a few
hours at room temperature.
AVAILABLE FROM: model shops in very small tins; most paint
merchants and ironmongers in larger quantities.
USE FOR: touching up METALS.

Gold leaf
This is real gold in very fine sheets.
AVAILABLE FROM: Fine art suppliers.
USE FOR: GILDING

Oil colours
These ordinary artists' oil paints are very slow drying. Mixed with linseed oil, they give a shinier finish; with turpentine, a duller one.
AVAILABLE FROM: artists' suppliers.

Pigment colours
These are pure ground colours used for mixing into artists' colours.
AVAILABLE FROM: artists' suppliers.

Poster (or Powder) colours
Powdered colours to be mixed with water, used primarily for hand-coloured posters, murals etc.
AVAILABLE FROM: artists' suppliers.

Stains
Translucent, usually aniline dyes in a spirit or oil solution, used to distribute colour on absorbent surfaces, such as wood, plaster and ceramic materials. Older, more limited stains in water solution are also used. Many have a chemical as well as a staining action. (see also under **Wood Stains**)
AVAILABLE FROM: ironmongers, DIY shops, and specialist suppliers.

Tempera
The traditional medium for miniature and very delicate fine paintings. Pure pigments are ground up and mixed with egg yolk to produce the paints.
AVAILABLE FROM: artists' suppliers.

Water colours
Ready-made pigment colours mixed with water and gum.
AVAILABLE FROM: artists' suppliers.

Dry cleaning agents – see **Solvents**.

Fillers
Fillers and stoppers, used to fill cracks and smooth out irregularities in all kinds of articles are an essential tool for the renovator and

restorer of antiques. A list, by no means exhaustive, of some of the available materials is given below.

Brummer stopper
This is a compound formulated in various colours specially for use in cabinet making. It is smooth, can be thinned with water, and does not shrink on drying. It, and similar products, are favoured for stopping cracks and small holes when renovating furniture.
AVAILABLE FROM: ironmongers.
USE FOR: BONE, FURNITURE, PAPIER MACHE.

Dental plaster
This is a superior version of Plaster of Paris (see below), and is sometimes used for repairing ceramics. Its main use is for repairing gesso-based frames, as it is an ideal material for casting into small details which are missing from gilt and painted carving. Water can destroy it in time.
AVAILABLE FROM: Dental suppliers (Ask your dentist).
USE FOR: CERAMICS, GESSO-BASED FRAMES, GILT CARVING.

Epoxy Resin putty
This material is the first choice for the repair of all kinds of ceramics, having superseded such materials as Barbola paste. It can also be used for modelling missing parts, and as a filler for cracks and holes in stoneware, marble etc. It is available in two-part, ready-to-mix containers. The putty is white, but can be coloured with poster colour, or better still, painted when dry.
   As an alternative to the proprietary brand, you can make your own putty using epoxy resin adhesive mixed with French chalk or kaolin or, if the body of the article to be repaired is brilliant white, with Titanium Oxide (available from art shops). Small chips and holes are easy to model in, but larger areas to be filled will need support while the putty is drying.
BEST KNOWN BRANDS: Sylmasta, Sylnicesta
AVAILABLE FROM: art shops, or write to the manufacturers: The Sylglas Company*, Frank W. Joel*
USE FOR: ALABASTER, BONE, CERAMICS, CHINA DOLLS, COMPOSITION

DOLLS, JADE, MARBLE, ONYX, PAPIER MACHE FURNITURE,
STONEWORK

Fibreglass (see below under *Plastic fillers*)

Gesso
Gesso is the base coat that is applied to wood or indeed any surface
that is to be gilded or painted. It fills in the cracks and the grain and
can be rubbed down to a perfect-blemish free surface. It is applied
by brush, coat on coat, until the desired surface is achieved. Thicker
Gesso is sometimes used for modelling in details, but the use of
other materials is quicker and easier.

Gesso can be purchased in most art suppliers, as it is used as a
foundation on canvasses, or it can be made up by mixing whiting to
a fine paste with water to remove all lumps. It should be the
consistency of thick cream and to this paste add enough carpenter's
glue (from the hot gluepot) to reduce the consistency to that of
pouring cream. To this add a few drops of Linseed Oil (about three
drops per eggcup full).

Broken and missing areas can then be built up again with
successive coats of Gesso. The repaired areas should be slightly
proud of the rest of the detail to allow for rubbing down when
thoroughly dry. Where original gesso has become detached or
loose, new Gesso can be worked underneath with a palette knife
and cracks can be similarly filled. The repair will dry marble-hard
and can be sandpapered or carved down to shape.
AVAILABLE FROM: art shops.

Grain fillers
These can be bought in both paste and liquid forms and are used for
making coarse-grained wood smooth before staining and finishing.
BEST KNOWN BRANDS: Rustin's grain filler, Signpost grain filler.
AVAILABLE FROM: most hardware shops and specialist supplier such
as Gedge* and Henry Flack*.
USE FOR: FURNITURE, FRAMES, PLASTER WORK.

Hard wax filler
Shrinkage and cracking often occurs on old furniture, even though it has been well looked after, and in consequence has acquired a beautiful patina that it would be a crime to disturb. On those and some other occasions the most sensible course to take is to fill the gaps with a suitably coloured Hard Wax Filler which will neither disturb the surface or in any way damage the valuable piece of furniture.

Hard waxes can be bought in sticks of various colours and are similar to sealing wax. The application technique is to heat up the tang of a file, or similar steel pointed tool and melt the wax by holding it on the hot metal, the melted wax will run down the tang and can be directed into the crack. After hardening off, but before completely cold, all excess wax can be trimmed off with a sharp chisel.
AVAILABLE FROM: Specialist suppliers, such as Gedge*, Flack*.
USE FOR: BOULLE, FURNITURE, TORTOISESHELL.

Plaster of Paris
Used for making castings of missing detail, and during the last century as a wood filler.
AVAILABLE FROM: Chemists and hospital suppliers.
USE FOR: CASTING

Plastic fillers (Fibreglass)
These are very useful for effecting repairs to wood that has been cut or chewed away to such an extent that original fittings, such as castors on the end of chair or table legs, can no longer be secured satisfactorily. The cavity can be packed with the filler and the part becomes cemented in. As these products are coloured, they can only be used where they are inconspicuous, or can be painted or otherwise concealed but they make an exceedingly firm repair.
BEST KNOWN BRANDS: Plastic Padding, Isopon.
AVAILABLE FROM: ironmongers, hardware shops, motorists' shops.
USE FOR: COMPOSITION DOLLS, FURNITURE

Plastic Wood (see below, under *Sawdust and carpenter's glue*)

Powder and paste fillers
These are excellent for a variety of purposes. Many nowadays are
plastic based and set rock hard. Some can be stained, so they can be
used for filling wood that is not going to be painted over, but read
the manufacturer's instructions.
BEST KNOWN BRANDS: Polyfilla, Tetrion, Moltogo Uni-Filler.
AVAILABLE FROM: ironmongers, decorating shops.
USE FOR: COMPOSITION DOLLS, LACQUERWARE, WOODWORM HOLES,
general filling.

Sawdust and carpenter's glue
This mixture, made to a mastic consistency, can be used to fill quite
large holes in damaged woodwork. Use sawdust of the same variety
of wood as the rest of the work and the repair becomes less visible.
It is a traditional repair material and is surprisingly strong and
durable. Plastic Wood is a commercially available version of this,
and is used for filling cracks and holes in woodwork. Not as much
favoured by professional cabinet-makers as other stoppers, but
universally available.
AVAILABLE FROM: DIY shops and ironmongers.

French polish
There are dozens of grades and qualities of French polish available
on the market (one London manufacturer lists 38), but for the
non-professional French polisher, the task is made an easy one by
using only one variety of French polish which is so versatile that it is
suitable for almost every occasion. This is Furniglas Home French
Polish, widely available in DIY packs. These contain two liquids: a
specially formulated French polish and a finishing, buffing and
hardening medium. Do not be put off by the adjective 'Home' – it is
better than most varieties available and is used by many
professional antique restorers. The only occasion when it is not
suitable to use is on very light wood, when Furniglas Colourless
Polish should be substituted.
    Do not be misled by various names like Button polish, Garnet
polish, White polish: these are only colour identifications. You will
find that Furniglas Home French Polish produces a hard and

durable finish, providing you follow the maker's instructions to the letter. Do not listen to the advice of even the expert who may have a 'secret tip' to pass on. There is a lot of 'magic' talked about French polishing, which is not, in reality, as difficult as it is made out to be.

For detailed instructions – see FURNITURE – FRENCH POLISHING. RECOMMENDED BRAND: Furniglas Home French Polish, Furniglas Colourless Polish.

AVAILABLE FROM: most DIY and hardware stores, or write to Furniglas Ltd*.

Fuller's earth

This is a type of clay which is found in various locations and which has the property of absorbing various oily and greasy substances. It is widely used commercially for cleaning fabrics and furs, where washing or otherwise wetting is inadvisable. It is normally used as a dry powder.

To remove grease spots from carpets, dust Fuller's earth all over the spotted area and leave for 24 hours, then brush away and vacuum clean. For delicate textiles and appliqué work, apply a Fuller's earth poultice made up by mixing it with cold water.

AVAILABLE FROM: most chemists.

USE FOR: APPLIQUE, CARPETS, FRAGILE FABRICS, FURS.

Fungicides

Fungus attack is almost always associated with damp conditions and can occur in a wide variety of hosts from paper to stonework. Elimination involves extermination of the spores and the removal of the source of moisture. Selecting a suitable fungicide depends on the degree of fragility of the article under attack. Killing the fungus does not automatically eliminate the stain which it has caused.

Formalin solution is a good all-round fungicide, while there are a number of proprietary brands of fungicidal liquids suitable for stone, plaster and the like.

Chloramine T should be used for delicate work, as well as the phenolic chemicals such as *Thymol* (which is soluble in solvent spirit) and can be used on both paper and fabric.

Potassium Permanganate is also a good fungicide, but it will cause

stains on delicate objects.
BEST KNOWN BRANDS: Formalin Solution, Blue Circle Fungicide.
AVAILABLE FROM: Chemists, or try builders' merchants for
fungicides suitable for stone and plaster. Frank W. Joel Ltd*

Furniture cleaners

Dull and lifeless surfaces can often be revived and brightened up,
and this involves cleaning down before waxing. Usually a thorough
scrub down with fine wire wool and White Spirit used as a solvent
will remove both accumulated dirt and old wax without damaging
any French Polish or varnish surface. Always rub the wire wool in
the direction of the grain of the wood and use only the finer grades
(000 grade is ideal).

Smeary surfaces can often be cured by less drastic methods, such
as wiping over with soft rag charged with vinegar and warm water,
followed by a burnishing with a chamois leather.

A good furniture cleaner can be made up as follows:

Linseed Oil	
Vinegar	4 parts of each
Real turpentine	
Methylated spirit	1 part

This mixture can be rubbed over the surface, but use it sparingly
until you have developed a familiarity with its use. Methylated spirit
melts French Polish, so an excess of the cleaner left on a polished
surface for too long will do more harm than good.

Furniture polishes

The ideal finish for any piece of natural wood furniture is a deep
glowing wax polish. In order to achieve this the best method is to
use a solid wax polish containing a high proportion of beeswax.
While it is easy to make up your own wax polish (a recipe is given
under **wax polishes**) it may be prudent to consider that the time that
will be required to achieve the requisite shine will outweigh the
money saved on proprietary polishes.

There is a wide choice of polishes on the market that their

manufacturers have spent years of research in perfecting. They contain a blend of hard waxes and quick solvents which produce a quick durable shine. Select one of the solid brands that the maker recommends for use on antique furniture. You will find that they are produced in a range of colours from clear to dark brown, so if you want to tone a piece of furniture the coloured waxes should be selected.

Furniture creams and oils are designed for removing surface dust and cleaning furniture, or for use on modern furniture that has a sprayed synthetic surface, so do not use it on antiques. Aerosols are a waste of money, even if they are easy to use. The bulk of the contents is propellant gas that polishes nothing.

Wax polish should be liberally applied three or four times a year. The rest of the time burnishing with a soft cloth is all that needs doing. An old short-haired paintbrush or a shoe-brush is a useful applicator for carved furniture. Cover the entire surface before going back to start polishing with a soft cloth. As the shine begins to appear, change over to a clean cloth and rub only in the direction of the grain.

If you encounter scratches, these can often be concealed and polished away by applying the right shade of boot polish. This is a tip widely used in the antique and modern furniture trades and is very effective. Another useful hint is to polish over brass handles and other fittings with wax polish. This will seal the surface so that oxidization is retarded and the brass stays bright.

Rings marks, heat marks and alcohol stains can sometimes be polished out if the damage has not penetrated too deep, there is, however, no magic wand that you can wave. All remedies consist of either mild abrasives, diluted solvents or a combination of both. There are again a number of ready made cures at the ironmongers, such as Topp's Ringaway or Furniglas No. 2 (part of their French Polishing Pack). Other alternatives are metal polish (Brasso or Silvo), cigar or cigarette ash and spittle, and as an extreme measure, fine wire wool lubricated with linseed oil or furniture polish. Where the stain has penetrated to the wood, the whole surface will have to be stripped and refinished, so consult a specialist.

BEST KNOWN BRANDS: Goddard's Antiquax, Gedge's range; Johnson wax (original with beeswax).

Insecticides
Insects will infest stuffed animals, carpets, wallhangings, books and
wood. But nowadays infestations can safely be prevented and
controlled with the use of a wide range of insecticides, many of
which are long-lasting in their effects. Should you find it difficult,
however, to eradicate infestations, most local authorities will advise
on how to clear them, and there are also a number of private pest
control operators working in most areas, who will undertake
fumigation (which is sometimes the only solution), so look in your
Yellow Pages.
   Insecticides are available in a number of forms:

Aerosols
These are the most convenient to use, but are relatively expensive,
as the carrier is normally an inert gas which propels atomised
insecticide on to the article to be treated.

Dusting powders
These are very effective for spreading underneath carpets and rugs
made of animal fibres (insects do not attack man-made fibres). They
contain only small percentages of active ingredient extended by
addition to inert powder.

Emulsions
Or, more correctly, emulsifiable concentrates which are diluted with
water and turn milky. These, after dilution, are normally odour free
and leave no visible deposit when dry, providing they are applied
with a fine mist-producing sprayer.

Mothballs and crystals
The most widely used component is Paradichlorobenzene. Apart
from their most obvious use of protecting fabrics in drawers, they
can also be scattered along the backs of bookshelves as a protection
against bookworms, silverfish, book-boring beetles and firebrats.

Solutions
Some insecticides are sold in a solution of white spirit or other
solvent. They contain low percentages of active ingredient and are

used without further dilution. The residue of insecticide is virtually invisible and does not stain.

Wettable powders
These products contain a higher proportion of active ingredient mixed with grinding and suspending agents, and are diluted by mixing with water into a suspension. This had to be agitated from time to time to prevent the particles from sinking to the bottom of the spraying machine. They leave a fine white deposit.

The most commonly encountered household insecticides are based on either Lindane B.H.C., Chlordane Pyrethrum or Diazinon. They are selected and labelled as being suitable for specific purposes by the manufacturer, but will exterminate or control a wide range of insect pests. Some pests, however, are notoriously difficult to control (such as carpet beetles), and in such cases professional assistance should be sought.

BEST KNOWN BRANDS: Cooper's insecticides, ICI household insecticides, Murphy Chemicals.

AVAILABLE FROM: chemists, ironmongers, supermarkets.

Woodworm control
Woodworm is the lava of the furniture beetle. The adult insect lays its eggs on suitable end-grain or other protected wood where they hatch into minute caterpillars which bore their way into the timber, forming galleries like miniature tubes. Eventually they pupate just below the surface, waiting for spring when they hatch into adult beetles which bite their way out, leaving behind a neat round exit hole. This hatch and emergence takes place in early spring each year.

The adult insect has only a short life of a few days, so the method of permanent protection is to apply a long-lasting insecticide which is both poisonous to the feeding grub and repellent to the adult female (who will not lay eggs on treated wood). The best time to apply the treatment is in early spring, before emergence, but any time will do. Woodworm treatments are sold as solutions of suitable chemicals in a solvent which will not harm furniture. Apply by brush or spray, taking care to treat all surfaces, both interior and exterior.

There will most likely be an emergence of beetles the following spring, because the treatment will not penetrate all the galleries, but do not worry; the adult beetles, if they survive, will not lay their eggs on treated timber.

BEST KNOWN BRANDS: Rentokil, Wyckemol.

AVAILABLE FROM: most ironmongers. Boots the Chemists also stock them.

Lacquer removers

Many metal objects, such as brass handles and wrought iron or copper fittings, used to be lacquered, and the lacquer has either gone dark with age or parts have peeled off. In spite of this deterioration the coating is likely to be extremely tenacious and impervious to normal metal cleaners.

Perhaps the most efficient lacquer remover is a good paint stripper.

It is essential to remove brass fittings from furniture etc. before using stripper and it is usually easier to immerse the pieces completely in the chemical, washing them thoroughly on removal under a running tap. Too long a soaking may etch the surface, so check from time to time, but a shine can be restored with polishing. If you have a buffing attachment to your electric drill, this will save time.

BEST KNOWN BRAND: Nitromors.

AVAILABLE FROM: most DIY stores, for Nitromors, or write direct to T.A. Hutchinson Ltd* for their own brand.

Leather treatments

British Museum Leather Dressing

This preparation was developed for the preservation and revival of antique leather articles. The formula is as follows, and the ingredients can be purchased from most chemists.

Hexane	11 fl. oz.
Beeswax	$\frac{1}{2}$ oz.
Anhydrous Lanolin	7 oz.
Cedarwood Oil	1 fl. oz.

Hexane is highly flammable. Dissolve the wax in the Hexane and then add the lanolin and the cedarwood oil. Mix well. Apply sparingly and rub well into the leather. After two days burnish with a duster.

It is also obtainable readymade.

AVAILABLE FROM: F.W. Joel Ltd*, Russell Bookcrafts*, Boots the Chemists (122 King's Road, London SW3 only).

Fortificuir
This is a patent leather dressing that both cleans and preserves all kinds of leather.

AVAILABLE FROM: Alfred Maltby and Son Ltd*.

Saddle soap
Saddle soap is a product often overlooked for the preservation of other leather articles than saddlery.

It has a cleansing as well as a polishing action, and on most leather articles it can be used with absolute safety. As it is used in conjunction with small quantities of water, care must obviously be taken when cleaning the covers of books or other articles where water would cause damage, but for such things as military accoutrements, antique luggage etc. it is an extremely useful material.

BEST KNOWN BRAND: Propert's Saddle Soap.

AVAILABLE FROM: most saddlers and shoe shops.

Metal cleaners
Brasso
Badly tarnished brass and copper respond well to a rubbing with wire wool impregnated with Brasso.

AVAILABLE FROM: ironmongers, hardware stores.

USE FOR: BRASS, COPPER.

Cubrite
This removes corrosion from brass and copper.

AVAILABLE FROM: Frank W. Joel Ltd*

USE FOR: Brass, copper

Horolene
This should be used diluted with water, and the article immersed in
the solution for at least 24 hours.
OBTAINABLE FROM: watch repairers, watchmakers' suppliers, or
direct from the manufacturers: Horological Solvents Ltd*.
USE FOR: BRASS FITTINGS, CLOCKS, COPPER, SCIENTIFIC
INSTRUMENTS, WATCHES.

Jenolite
(For a description see under **Rust removers**)
AVAILABLE FROM: ironmongers, garages.
USE FOR: rust removal from ALUMINIUM, BRASS, CHROME, COPPER,
IRON, STEEL.

Paraffin oil
To clean iron and steel use fine wire wool dipped in paraffin oil.
Immerse corroded pewter in paraffin oil. It may take anything from
a few hours to several days to clear away. Dry off with old
newspaper and wash in warm soapy water.
USE FOR: IRON, PEWTER, STEEL.

Silver Dip
This is a proprietary silver and jewellery cleaner generally available
from ironmongers and is ideal for cleaning small silver items. Larger
items can be cleaned by wiping with cotton-wool soaked in Silver
Dip and then rinsed.
   You can make your own silver dip by putting a square of
aluminium foil into the bottom of a plastic bowl, filling it with hot
water and adding several heaped tablespoons of washing soda. Put
the pieces of silver into the bowl immediately, while the solution is
effervescing, making sure they are completely covered. When the
bubbles stop the chemical action is over and the articles should be
washed in clean water and dried.

Metal cleaners (specialised applications only)
Acetic acid
Acetic acid is the chemical present in vinegar. It is usually used in a

Before and after, using Goddard's Silver Dip on a spoon

10% solution and can be bought in colourless form from chemists. To remove chlorine stains from bronze, use a 10% solution. Paint the liquid on the affected areas, which must be kept damp to allow the acid to get to work. Clean off by scrubbing the surface with a soft brush.

AVAILABLE FROM: chemists, or grocers (as vinegar).
USE FOR: stains on BRONZE.

Ammonia 🔥
(For a description see under **Bleaching agents**)

To remove advanced oxidization on pewter, soak in a bath of water and ammonia solution, but watch carefully that over-exposure does not damage the patina. Wash thoroughly after removal.
AVAILABLE FROM: chemists and ironmongers.
USE FOR: badly oxidized PEWTER.

Nitric acid 🔥
Dip copper coins in a 5% to 10% solution of nitric acid in water for a few seconds. Rinse immediately in a bowl of water.
AVAILABLE FROM: Chemists
USE FOR: COPPER.

Metal polishes
Proprietary metal polishes fall into three groups: de-tarnishers, polishers, and polishers with long-term protection against tarnishing. Goddard's Silver Dip is an excellent de-tarnisher for small items. Polish larger objects with their Long Term Silver Polish or Long Term Silver Foam. Such products incorporate a chemical tarnish barrier, harmless and invisible, which reduces the frequency of cleaning. You can make your own silver polish with a base of French Chalk made into a paste by adding methylated spirits and ammonia. It is best to use cotton-wool rather than a cloth to avoid minute scratching.

Iron and steel can be polished to a high finish with the finest grades of Jewellers' Emery Paper (see **Abrasives**). To bring an even higher finish to steel use Pink Porthos. It is used to dress a revolving cotton buffing wheel, and is the best and quickest material to make old ferrous articles gleam. You can also use Goddard's Stainless Steel Care on iron. For pewter, use Goddard's Glow, or a homemade recipe using Jeweller's rouge and salad oil.
BEST KNOWN BRANDS: Goddard's Silver Dip, Goddard's Long Term Silver Polish, Long Term Silver Foam, Stainless Steel Care, Goddard's Glow, Pink Porthos.
AVAILABLE FROM: most ironmongers and hardware stores for Goddard's products, also jeweller's for silver polishes; from metal finishing suppliers such as T.A. Hutchinson Ltd* for Pink Porthos.

Brasso – see under **Metal cleaners**

Oils and lubricants
Linseed oil
Linseed oil is one of the traditional materials for dressing and polishing wood. Throughout the eighteenth century the standard practice was to impregnate wood with a mixture of linseed oil and turpentine and burnish the surface with fine brick dust on a cork rubber.

Mixed with Shellac it was the basis of 'coach varnish'. Its use these days is confined to that of a reviver and ring remover on antique furniture, and a dressing to garden furniture made from raw unpainted wood. The practice of using a drop or two when applying the finishing coat of French Polish should be firmly discouraged, as it reduces the hardness of the finish.
AVAILABLE FROM: ironmongers, artists' suppliers.
USE FOR: FURNITURE

Molybendum disulphide
This non-oily lubricant is extremely useful for the protection of steel and other metal moving parts where an excess of oil is not desirable. It is used mostly for sporting guns but is useful generally for the protection of armour and weapons.
BEST KNOWN BRANDS: Dri-Slide, Molyslide.
AVAILABLE FROM: gunsmiths.
USE FOR: ARMOUR, GUNS, WEAPONS.

Paraffin oil
See under **Metal cleaners**

Penetrating oil
Penetrating oils have two main uses: loosening hard-to-shift nuts and bolts, and lifting off rust and corrosion. The simplest all-round kind is paraffin oil, but after its use for removal of rust, the article must be oiled; otherwise more rust will form. More sophisticated penetrating oils are also on sale, and they are an essential in any restorer's workshop.

BEST KNOWN BRANDS: Plus Gas, W.D.40.
AVAILABLE FROM: hardware stores, motor accessory shops.

Rifle oil
The traditional oil used on firearms, to keep them rust-free and in good working order, is Rangoon oil, although other alternatives are given below. Avoid using motor and heavy lubricating oils which may gum parts up.
BEST KNOWN BRANDS: Rangoon oil, 3-0-3, 3-in-one, Singer Machine Oil, Silicone Gun Oil 35.
AVAILABLE FROM: gunsmiths, or Abbey Supply Co* for Silicone Gun Oil
USE FOR: ARMOUR, FIREARMS, WEAPONS

Turpentine
This is the natural oily sap of certain types of pine tree. No longer used for mixing commercial paints, but still used for thinning and mixing artists' oil colours. Today it has very few uses except in the manufacture of wax furniture polishes and creams.

Ormolu cleaner
Cleaning ormolu can present some problems as the gold plating may be removed by too violent cleaning methods. The use of Horolene (see above) is favoured by most clock repairers when dealing with the not too large parts of an ormolu clock case.

The first thing always to do is to remove the ormolu decorations. This is not difficult; close examination will show that they are only attached by a few small brass screws or short dome headed tacks. The most easily available cleaner is likely to be ammonia, but if this is used, it is essential that the entire mount is totally submerged in the solution. Work over the surface with a soft brush and leave to soak for 10–15 minutes. On removal plunge *immediately* into a bath of water and then dry off.

Another recommended cleaning bath is:

Sodium Hydroxide	1 oz.
Sodium Potassium Tartrate	3 oz.
Water	1 quart.

Oxalic acid 🔥
see under **Bleaching agents**

Paint strippers

Over the last few years the effectiveness of most paint strippers has been greatly increased, but it is still important to understand the correct technique for using them to best effect. The commonest mistake made by those unfamiliar with stripping furniture etc. is to apply the stripper as if it were paint, and brush it out to produce a smooth surface. The only effect that this has is to reduce the efficiency of the stripper resulting in the need to apply more coats before the article is clean. Get as much of the stripper on to the article as will stick and leave it until the varnish or polish or paint has started to swell and cockle up.

Remove the first layer or so with a chisel scraper, taking care not to damage the surface of the wood. Several applications of stripper will be required to remove every vestige of the finish, and it is important that the article is absolutely clear of paint or varnish before starting to repolish.

When removing the last coat or two of stripper, a scraper will not be very effective and it should be replaced by a ball of the coarsest wire wool that you can obtain. The pad of wire wool should only be used in the direction of the grain; if you scrub across the grain you are likely to scratch the surface. Carving and awkward corners are best cleaned out with a combination of wire wool and sharpened and shaped pieces of scrap wood that will reach into the crevices.

After stripping has been completed, wipe over the surfaces thoroughly with white spirit to neutralise the residue of the stripper.

Nitromors is the most effective and most widely available paint stripper on the market. Two varieties are on sale, that in a green tin will remove plastic paints and hard enamels, but that in a yellow tin is quite effective for the removal of French Polish and Varnish. There are a number of proprietary brands supplied by specialist suppliers (see below).

Modern paint strippers will remove very nearly everything with the exception of Milk paint. (This was a home made product, popular in country districts during the 18th Century, and earlier, which was made by mixing boiled down buttermilk and animal blood.) The casein content renders it impervious to most paint strippers and the only solvent to which it is likely to respond is strong ammonia. This has to be scrubbed in with wire wool and left to soak. The resulting treacly mass can be washed and scraped off, again using wire wool to remove the last vestige.

If you are removing a thick Victorian finish (of either paint or varnish) remove the first few layers with a chisel scraper, the kind used for taking off wallpaper. Hold folded sheets of newspaper horizontally in one hand at the edge of the area being stripped and so collect the gunge before it drips on to the floor.

BEST KNOWN BRANDS: Nitromors.

AVAILABLE FROM: hardware stores and ironmongers, proprietary brands available from Gedge & Co* and Henry Flack Ltd*.

Polyurethane lacquers – see under **Varnishes and lacquers**

Rust, tarnish and verdigris removers
A revolution has taken place in the mediums that can be employed to rid ferrous articles of rust, and there are now a number of compounds on the market to remove and inhibit rust.

They are based on phosphoric acid formulations that both destroy and remove rust, leaving behind a coating of inert iron phosphate which is a positive corrosion inhibitor. They are available in both liquid and jelly formulations for either brush or spot application. In some, waxes are incorporated to deposit an impervious semi-permanent protective coat.

BEST KNOWN BRANDS: Jenolite, Movol Rusteater.

AVAILABLE FROM: Motor accessory shops, ironmongers. In case of difficulty write to Frank W. Joel Ltd*.

Solvents
'Solvents', as far as we are concerned, is the loose term applied to liquids that can be used to loosen or wash off all kinds of dirt and grease. Of course, water is a solvent, but for our purpose we exclude it and concentrate on the commoner highly volatile liquids.

Acetone 🔥
This is a rapid solvent of cellulose paints and glues, and is useful as a general cleaning fluid. It is highly flammable and should be used only under well-ventilated conditions as the vapour is dangerous to inhale.
AVAILABLE FROM: chemists.
USE FOR: ENAMELLED WARE.

Alcohol
This is most widely used as a solvent under the name of Methylated Spirit. This is methyl alcohol which has been debased with dye and other noxious substances to make it undrinkable. It has a wide application for removing grease, oil and associated grime. It also mixes with water and can be used for accelerated drying and the removal of moisture. It is the basic solvent for French polish and will dissolve French polished and some varnished surfaces. To avoid staining, use uncoloured spirit (surgical spirit).
AVAILABLE FROM: chemists.

Benzene 🔥
This is similar to petrol, but is produced as a by-product of distilling coal. It is a good general cleaner, but is flammable and the fumes should not be inhaled.
AVAILABLE FROM: most chemists.
USE FOR: removal of grease stains from PAPER

Carbon Tetrachloride
This is a common non-flammable solvent. However, avoid smoking or naked flames in close proximity, as this will produce poisonous fumes. Use only under well-ventilated conditions. It is an excellent dry-cleaning fluid.

AVAILABLE FROM: chemists (sold under different trade names as dry cleaning fluid).
USE FOR: APPLIQUE, EMBROIDERY, ENAMELLED WARE, FABRICS, PAPER, SILVER COINS

Methylated spirit – see *Alcohol* above

Odourless kerosene – see *White spirit* below

Surgical spirit – see *Alcohol* above

Trichloroethane 🔥
Use this in conjunction with spirit soap (½ oz to two pints of the solvent).
AVAILABLE FROM: most chemists.
USE FOR: FABRICS, LEATHER.

Turps substitute – see *White spirit* below

White spirit
Sometimes called Turps Substitute or Odourless Kerosene, this is widely used as a dry cleaning spirit, mixed with other more volatile solvents. It is safer to use than most other solvents, although it will burn. It is a good grease, oil and dirt solvent and does not attack French polish or varnish, so can be used to clean off superficial dirt without attacking the base polish. It is useful for dewaxing furniture which will not burnish up. Kerosene or paraffin is a cruder and smellier form of white spirit which is more effective as a rust remover.
AVAILABLE FROM: ironmongers, chemists.
USE FOR: cleaning and dewaxing FURNITURE.

Xylene 🔥
This is a powerful solvent which will remove all kinds of dirt and grease. It is flammable and more expensive than the commoner solvents, but is often more effective at removing stains from textiles than anything else.
AVAILABLE FROM: chemists.
USE FOR: FABRICS.

Stain removers
Acetic acid
This is the chemical present in vinegar. It is usually used in a 10% solution, and can be bought colourless. Its principal use in restoration is to remove stains from prints and paper. It will also restore fabric colours.
AVAILABLE FROM: chemists.
USE FOR: FABRICS, PAPER.

Oxalic acid 🔥
This chemical (which is poisonous) is used principally to remove ink, and other stains from woodwork. It can be bought as a white crystalline powder and made into a saturated solution by dissolving as much as will in hot water. The solution is then flooded on to the stained surface and scrubbed in with wire wool. On most furniture the whole surface must be treated; otherwise you will run the risk of being left with a light patch where the ink stains used to be.
The area should be neutralised by thorough washing with clean water before being set aside to dry. It will also remove rust, and other stains from fabrics and leather, but here should be used in a 50% solution (i.e., half water, half saturated solution).
AVAILABLE FROM: chemists.
USE FOR: FABRICS, FURNITURE, LEATHER.

Stone cleaners, sealers and polishers
There are three stages involved in repairing stonework, though of course not all are necessarily needed at the same time: cleaning, sealing, and polishing. A Northampton firm, A. Bell & Co Ltd, supply direct the best materials for all stages.

No 1. Bell 1967 cleaner
A multi-purpose cleaner and degreaser for all materials and general household use (floors, ovens, paintwork etc).

No 2. Bell Marble Polish
A good all-round wax polish where a tough surface is required. Use sparingly (or thin with pure turpentine).

No 3. Belsealer
A first-class sealer for all slightly porous surfaces. It renders the surface impervious to oil, dust, and dirt, and brings out to a remarkable degree the colour and patterns of the material – particularly of Northamptonshire and 'Muresque' stones. Natural slate should be lightly treated. Very porous material may need two treatments.

No 4. Bell 'Two-Pack' General Cleaner for Floors
This contains: $\frac{1}{2}$ pint each of Nos 1 and 3 and can be used on stone, slate or tiled floors.

No 6. Bell Marble 'Touch Up' Pack
This contains garnet paper for rubbing down and lacquer for touching up polished marble where small areas of the polished surface have been chipped or damaged.

No 7. Bell Special Marble Cleaner
This is specially produced for rustic and honed marble, polished marble and stained vitreous enamel.

No. 8. Bell 1966 Cleaner
A powerful cleaner for stone only. It removes plaster and cement from the surface.

No 9. Bell Oil Stain Remover
A caustic, inflammable compound which acts upon oil and grease stains absorbed in concrete, natural stones and slates or porous surfaces.
AVAILABLE FROM: A. Bell & Co Ltd*.

Varnishes and lacquers
Acrylic and P.V.A. lacquers
These modern 'plastic' products have superseded the older Shellac based varnishes. They are clear, durable and long lasting. Most can be purchased in either gloss or matt finish. Fine art varieties are available for varnishing pictures.

They should be used to cover acrylic paints.

AVAILABLE FROM: artists' suppliers.

USE FOR: sealing almost anything.

Polyurethane lacquers

There are three types of finish available (gloss, satin or semi-matt, and matt). Remember that any varnish will slightly darken the shade of light woods. They provide a tough, impermeable finish, resistant to heat, abrasion and most common chemicals. Apply with a brush, using even strokes. They are dry-touch hard in four to six hours. If you brush them out well so that only a thin coat is applied, there will be no brush-marks, but is is wise to apply at least three coats; sand down the first coat, which serves as a grain filler and sealer.

BEST KNOWN BRANDS: Furniglas P.U.15, Rustin's Polyurethane Varnish, Ronseal Clear Polyurethane Varnish, Humbrol Clear Polyurethane.

AVAILABLE FROM: Builders' merchants, DIY shops, ironmongers.

USE FOR: BAMBOO, BASKETWORK, ENAMELWARE, FURNITURE, PAPIER-MACHE.

Veneers

The laying of large areas of veneer by traditional methods with Scotch glue and a veneering hammer is the work of a specialist. However, using modern impact adhesives, particularly those that allow for a little movement like Dunlop Thiofix or Evostik Time Bond, this task can be undertaken by a novice. Veneers can be bought from specialist merchants (see below), or if only very small quantities are required you can buy a marquetry set which will contain a variety of small pieces of veneers of various shades and textures. See also FURNITURE REPAIRS – VENEER.

Small repairs involving patching can be done with any of the normal wood glues but larger areas will expand and wrinkle if water-based glues are employed.

AVAILABLE FROM: Veneer merchants (see Yellow Pages) or direct from Crispin & Son Ltd*.

Wax polishes

When choosing a polish for furniture or other wooden or metal objects, always use a solid product containing a combination of beeswax with other hard vegetable waxes like Carnauba wax. There are a large number of proprietary brands on the market which you can choose from. Polishes are available in clear or tinted form. Antique effects can be obtained by using the latter, which are suitable for modern and antique furniture alike. Various shades of bootpolish can also be used to conceal and cover scratches and minor blemishes on a variety of surfaces.

BEST KNOWN BRANDS: Goddard's Cabinet Makers' Wax, Antiquax, Renaissance Wax Polish, Ronuk Wax Polish.

AVAILABLE FROM: hardware stores, or both Gedge & Co* and Henry Flack* also make their own brands which are only obtainable direct.

Beeswax polish

Shred about a pound of beeswax on a vegetable shredder and pack lightly into a double boiler. Add sufficient real turpentine to just cover the lightly packed flakes of wax and enough carbon black to cover a penny piece.

Heat carefully and when liquid stir to distribute the constitutents evenly. Pour into a suitable container to cool and harden. It should be soft enough for you to be able to stick your finger into the finished polish, leaving a permanent indentation.

Bell Marble polish – see under **Stone cleaners, sealers and polishes**

British Museum Leather Dressing – see under **Leather Treatments**

Microcrystalline wax polish

This preparation is widely used, and is recommended by museums for the preservation of a large range of antique objects made from bisque, metal, leather, stone and wood. Due to the white spirit content, it has a cleansing action in addition to the protective layer of wax which is deposited on the surface of the treated object. It is available ready-made, or you can make it up as follows:

Cosmolloid wax 80 hard	100 grammes
BASF wax A	25 grammes
White spirit	300 millilitres

Melt the wax and pour into the white spirit.
BEST KNOWN BRAND: Renaissance wax.
AVAILABLE FROM: ironmongers, artists' suppliers such as Alec
Tiranti*, Frank W. Joel Ltd*, or direct from the makers: Picreator
Enterprises Ltd*.
USE FOR: BISQUE, LEATHER, METAL, STONE, WOOD.

Wood finishing materials

With antique articles made of wood the complete technique of
wood finishing is unnecessary, indeed it could be damaging. All that
is normally required is resurfacing and repolishing, for all that
usually deteriorates is the old finishing coats of either varnish,
French polish, lacquer or even just old, tired wax. Once this old
surfacing has been removed – and every last scrap of polish or
varnish must be stripped – the filling of the wood and much or all of
the colouring will remain.

Some light spirit stain may be required to restore fading,
particularly on top surfaces, followed by repolishing. Often all that
is needed is a thorough coating of a suitable wax furniture polish.
The alternatives are a light French polishing or one or two coats of
one of the new-style clear varnishes such as Ronseal or Furniglas
PU15. In either case a finishing coat of wax polish is desirable.

For full details refer to the sections dealing with FURNITURE –
FRENCH POLISHING, **French polish, Varnishes and lacquers**, and
Wax polishes.

Wood stains
Traditional methods
Traditionally wood stains were water-based and most had a
chemical as well as a colouring action. Water stains have the
disadvantage of being slow to dry and of raising the grain of the
wood. Their advantage is that they are fast, non-fading colours.

Ammonia imparts a rich red colour to mahogany and some other woods. These days it is applied in liquid form rather than the traditional 'fuming'.

Brunswick produces a variety of pinks and scarlets, depending on the strength of the solution.

Caustic Soda turns pine and some other light woods greyish and produces a mid-brown in elm and oak.

Potassium Bichromate, though naturally orange, has a chemical action which develops to a honey-brown after an hour or so on most furniture woods.

Turmeric is a yellow stain.

Vandyke crystals produce a cold dark brown.

Tones are shaded in with pigments such as lamp black and red lead, which are the two most favoured traditional ones.

AVAILABLE FROM: specialist suppliers such as Flack*, Gedge*.

Anilyne dyes

Used in solvent spirit such as naptha or methylated spirit 🔥 , these ready-mix stains are quick and easy to apply. Colours range from Golden Oak to Brown Walnut and Dark Oak. Do not try to get the shade you want in one application, but start with a light shade and work the wood up to the shade you require by multiple applications of various kinds of stain. Do not be misled by the different names of wood used by the manufacturer to identify colours; they are only descriptive and do not relate to the wood to which they are applied.

BEST KNOWN BRANDS: Coloron, Rustin's.

AVAILABLE FROM: ironmongers, or Gedge & Co* for their own brand.

USE FOR: BONE, BASKETWORK, CANEWORK, FURNITURE, WOOD.

Pigment, powder colours

These are useful for making up more concentrated solutions for painting in grain configuration, dark patches or shading where the ready-made stains do not give the desired effect.

AVAILABLE FROM: artists' suppliers.

Section Three:
Index of suppliers

Note: All the firms listed supply by mail order, except those marked
NMO.

The Abbey Supply Co.   (RIFLE OIL)
6 Mill Lane
Wallingford, Oxon.

Afrasian Imports   (SHELLS)
2 Kneesworth Street
Royston
Herts

Altrincham Rubber Co.   (ELASTIC)
The Downs
Altrincham
Cheshire

Antique Leathers Ltd   (TABLE LEATHERS)
4 Park End
South Hill Park
London N.W.3

Ashley Iles (Edge Tools) Ltd   (CARVING TOOLS AND CHISELS)
East Kirkby
Spilsby
Lincs

W. Beal & Partners   (TABLE LEATHERS)
2 Whites Grounds
Bermondsey Street
London S.E.1

J.D. Beardmore & Co. Ltd   (BRASS HANDLES AND FITTINGS)
3 Percy Street
London W.1

A. Bell & Co. Ltd   (STONE CLEANING MATERIALS)
Kingsthorpe Works
Northampton
NN2 6LT

John Boyd   (HORSE HAIR FABRICS)
Castle Cary
Nr Yeovil
Somerset

R. Clements Upholstery   (TABLE LEATHERS)
50 Fullers Road
London E.15

Copydex Ltd   (STRONG TAPE)
1 Torquay Street
Harrow Road
London W.2

CoSIRA   (A GOVERNMENT BODY WHICH
Queens House   ASSISTS CRAFTSMEN IN
Fish Row   FURNITURE MAKING,
Salisbury   BLACKSMITHING, BASKETRY,
Wilts SP1 1EX   LEATHER WORKING. There is a
                              CoSIRA representative in almost
                              every county who will assist you
                              in finding suitable craft workers
                                 for restoration work.)

Crafts Unlimited   (INCLUDING CANE, GENERAL CRAFT SUPPLIERS)
178 Kensington High Street
London W.8

Crispin & Son Ltd   (STRINGING-WOOD, VENEERS, INLAYS)
92 Curtain Road
London E.C.2

Deben Craftsmen
11c St Peter's St
Ipswich, Suffolk

40 Dover Books   (DOLLS' HOUSE WALLPAPER, FLOOR COVERING)
10 Orange St
London WC2H 7EG

Dryad Handicrafts   (GENERAL CRAFT SUPPLIERS, INCLUDING CANE)
Northgates
Leicester LE1 9BU

Eastons Shell Shop   (SHELLS)
16 Manette Street
London W.1

Ellis & Farrier Ltd   (BEADS AND SEQUINS)
5 Princess Street
London WIR 8PH

Escaré Metal Co. Ltd   (BRASS CASTINGS)
195 Bexhill Road
St Leonards on Sea
E. Sussex.

Fiddes & Son   (FRENCH POLISHING SUNDRIES)
Trade Street
Cardiff
Glamorgan

Henry Flack Ltd   (FRENCH POLISHING SUNDRIES)
Croydon Road
Beckenham
Kent

NMO Furniglas Ltd   (FRENCH POLISH)
     136 Great North Road
     Hatfield
     Herts

NMO Garner & Marney Ltd   (BAROMETER PARTS AND REPAIRS)
     41 Southgate Road
     London N.1

     Gedge & Co. Ltd   (FRENCH POLISHING SUNDRIES)
     88 St John Street
     London E.C.1

     Grainwave Enterprises   (LEATHER)
     15 Clifton Gardens
     London N.15

     Handicrafts (Peterborough) Ltd   (PICTURE FRAMING MATERIALS)
     New Road
     Peterborough
     Cambs

     Keith Harding Ltd   (MUSIC BOX REPAIRS AND PARTS)
     93 Hornsey Road
     London N.7

NMO J. Hewitt & Sons   (BOOKBINDING SUPPLIES)
     97 St John Street
     London E.C.1

     W. Hobby Ltd   (DOLLS' HOUSE FURNITURE)
     Knights Hill Square
     London S.E.27

     Hobby Horse   (BEADS AND SEQUINS)
     15–17 Langton Street
     London S.W.10

Horological Solvents Ltd   (HOROLENE)
Bury
Lancs

T.A. Hutchinson Ltd   (METAL POLISHING MATERIALS)
16 St John's Lane
London E.C.1

In Flower   (FEATHERS)
Sherborne
Dorset

W.S. Jenkins Ltd   (FRENCH POLISHING SUPPLIES,
Tauff Road   CARPENTER'S GLUE, WOOD BLEACHES)
London N17 OE1

F.W. Joel Ltd   (SOLVENTS, METAL CLEANERS)
Oldmedow Road
Hardwick Industrial Estate
King's Lynn,
Norfolk PE30 4HH.

John Lawrence & Co. Ltd   (BRASS HANDLES AND FITTINGS)
Granville Street
Dover
Kent

Arthur Lee & Son   (TAPESTRY)
Stanley Road
Birkenhead
Cheshire

Loctite U.K. Ltd   (ADHESIVES)
Welwyn Garden City
Herts AL7 1JB

Mace & Nairn   (LACEMAKING SUPPLIES)
89 Crane Street
Salisbury
Wilts

T. Marten & Sons Ltd   (CHAIN BURNISHERS)
Bridgeman Street
Walsall
Staffs

Mobilia   (UPHOLSTERY SUPPLIES)
44 Henniker Road
Stratford
London E.15

Music Box Society   (MUSIC BOX REPAIRS AND PARTS)
Bylands
Crockham Hill
Edenbridge
Kent

Paperchase Products Ltd   (PAPER, LINING, COLOURED ETC)
216 Tottenham Court Road
Lond W.1

Pater Textiles Ltd   (TEXTILES)
Rampart Street
London E.1

Picreator Enterprises Ltd
44 Park View Gardens
London NW14

E. Ploton (Sundries) Ltd   (GILDING SUPPLIES AND LEAF)
273 Archway Road
London N.6

Pollock's Toy Museum   (DOLLS' LIMBS, HEADS, EYES)
Scala Street
London W.1

Reckitt & Colman   (ZEBRITE BLACKLEAD)
P.O. Box 26
1/17 Burlington Lane
London W4 2RW

Regina Fabrics   (TEXTILES)
40–42 Great Eastern Street
London E.C.2

Russell Bookcrafts   (BOOKBINDING SUPPLIES)
Bancroft
Hitchin
Herts

H.E. Saville   (BRASS HANDLES AND FITTINGS)
Sunwood
Weaponness Park
Scarborough
Yorks

Semnat Glass Works Ltd   (ANTIQUED MIRRORS)
73 Hackney Road
London E.2

Smith & Son Ltd   (BRASS INLAY, STRIP AND SHEET)
42–52 St John Square
London E.C.1

Strand Glassfibre Ltd   (MOULDING SUPPLIES)
Brentway Trading Estate
Brentford
Middlesex

The Sylglas Co.   (SYLMASTA)
Denso House
Chapel Road
London SE27 ORT

Taylor & Co. Ltd   (LEATHER)
54 Old Street
London E.C.1

Henry Taylor   (CARVING TOOLS AND CHISELS)
Rutland Road
Sheffield
S3 9NP

Alec Tiranti Ltd   (MOULDING, CASTING SUPPLIES,
70 High Street   CARVING TOOLS AND CHISELS)
Theale
Berks
and 21 Goodge Place
London W.1

Unibond Ltd   (WOOD ADHESIVES)
Tuscan Way
Camberley
Surrey

Watts & Co. Ltd   (NEEDLEWORK SUNDRIES)
7 Tufton Street
London S.W.1

Geo. Whiley Ltd   (GILDING SUPPLIES AND LEAF)
Victoria Road
South Ruislip
Middlesex

World of Wood   (WOOD AND WOODWORKING REQUISITES)
Industrial Estate
Mildenhall
Suffolk

Christopher Wray's   (LAMP GLASSES AND SUNDRIES)
Lighting Emporium
600 King's Road
London SW6 2DX